Creative Development in the Early Years Foundation Stage

The clear and practical information in this book will help practitioners in supporting and developing the natural curiosity of children, helping them explore and express their own ideas through a variety of activities including music art and dance. The author explores the balance between the necessary freedoms of choice that creativity requires and the control which thoughtful practitioners must exert and offers ideas for building children's imaginations through play.

Pam May is an Early Years consultant.

Practical Guidance in the EYFS
Series Editor: Sandy Green

The *Practical Guidance in the EYFS* series will assist practitioners in the smooth and successful implementation of the Early Years Foundation Stage.

Each book gives clear and detailed explanations of each aspect of learning and development and encourages readers to consider each area within its broadest context to expand and develop their own knowledge and good practice.

Practical ideas and activities for all age groups are offered along with a wealth of expertise of how elements from the practice guidance can be implemented within all early years' settings. The books include suggestions for the innovative use of everyday resources, popular books and stories.

Creative Development in the Early Years Foundation Stage

Pamela May

Routledge
Taylor & Francis Group

LONDON AND NEW YORK

First published 2009
by Routledge
2 Park Square, Milton Park, Abingdon, Oxon OX14 4RN

Simultaneously published in the USA and Canada
by Routledge
270 Madison Avenue, New York, NY 10016

Routledge is an imprint of the Taylor & Francis Group, an informa business

© 2009 Pamela May

Typeset in Optima by
Taylor & Francis Books
Printed and bound in Great Britain by
TJ International Ltd, Padstow, Cornwall

British Library Cataloguing in Publication Data
A catalogue record for this book is available from the British Library

Library of Congress Cataloging in Publication Data
May, Pamela.
  Creative development in the early years foundation stage / Pamela May.
    p. cm.
  1. Creative thinking–Study and teaching (Early childhood) 2. Creative
  ability in children. 3. Child development. I. Title.
  LB1062.M38 2008
370.15′2–dc22   2008031889

ISBN 978-0-415-47836-6 (hbk)
ISBN 978-0-415-47653-9 (pbk)

Contents

These principles reflect children's rights to grow up safely and healthily and to achieve their potential through challenging but enjoyable learning experiences.

The EYFS places an increased emphasis on practitioners' understanding of child development so that learning experiences can be carefully matched to the individual child's interests, abilities and preferred ways of learning. There is also an emphasis on the vitally important role that children's families play in providing children with their first and continuing education.

A recognition of the close emotional links established between young children and primary carers, both at home and in the setting, is a key feature of this document; as is the requirement to match learning experiences to children by carefully 'looking, listening and noting' (DfES 2007). This places a high emphasis on planning, based on sound observation of children, to give a firm foundation on which to plan for and assess their next steps as well as their overall progress.

This book takes the creative-development area of the EYFS and aims to help practitioners reflect on their practice and to develop it so that all children can learn both about being creative and also how to learn in creative ways across the whole curriculum. It uses the strands and requirements of the EYFS, the commitments and areas of child development as its basic structure when exploring different aspects of creativity.

Creativity is one of the basic building blocks of the human species. Together with the necessity to be numerate, literate and to understand about and function within the world around us, creativity enables humans to function at their highest level; it engages curiosity, focuses concentration and stimulates feelings of well-being. To create something of which one is proud is one of the most deeply satisfying emotions that humans can experience and may well have its origins in the basic need of humans to adapt and change to survive.

In terms of young children's learning, creativity is closely linked to all the other areas of learning in the EYFS. Children need a good self-image to be creative and, conversely, creative children will enjoy innovative and lateral thinking whilst learning about numbers, language and science. They will give and receive great pleasure from what they create, be it through music, painting, construction or imaginative play.

Within the framework of the EYFS, this book explores the conditions that best support creativity in both children and in practitioners. It considers how the themes of the EYFS can be used to encourage creativity and how practitioners' accurate observations of children, their flexible use of resources

Introduction

The Early Years Foundation Stage (EYFS) gives a mandatory framework to providers of all registered early years settings. Its purpose is to enable children to achieve the five outcomes of *Every Child Matters* (DfES 2004), a central element of the Government's ten-year childcare strategy, *Choice for Parents, the Best Start for Children*. These outcomes are:

1 staying safe;
2 being healthy;
3 enjoying and achieving;
4 making a positive contribution;
5 achieving economic well-being.

The principles that underpin the EYFS are crucial in helping children to achieve the aims of *Every Child Matters,* and they run, like threads, throughout the document. These principles, which are also referred to as commitments, state what practitioners need to have firmly in their minds and to include in their day-to-day practice to ensure that children are able to achieve the Every Child Matters outcomes.

The principles are grouped into four themes in the EYFS which are:

1 a unique child;
2 positive relationships;
3 enabling environments;
4 learning and developing.

Acknowledgements

I would like to dedicate this book to my grandchildren Millie, Jacob, Daisy and Albert. They have given photographs of their creative learning and have also provided me with opportunities to put theory into practice!

I would like to thank Anne Nurse for taking some of the photographs and Professor Marjorie Goldsmith, Director of the Child and Family Center at the Rockefeller University in New York, for permission to use photographs of her artist's room. Thanks are also due to the staff and children of the early years settings that I visit whose valuable work has provided the inspiration for some of the ideas contained in this book.

I would also like to thank Peers Early Education Partnership (PEEP) for permission to print the song 'Ready and ...' and to acknowledge the ways in which their creative resources support children's literacy development.

My thanks are due to my family for their continued love and encouragement and in particular to John May for his editorial support.

Every effort has been made to trace copyright holders of material reproduced in this book. Any right not acknowledged here will be acknowledged in subsequent printings if notice is given to the publishers.

and their knowledge of child development can help children to feel confident enough to express their creative and imaginative ideas. The EYFS Practice Guidance explains this concept beautifully. It suggests that children must *feel secure enough* to 'have a go', learn new things and be adventurous (DfES 2007: 104).

Each chapter in this book takes one of the aspects of the EYFS areas of learning known as creative development. For example, the first aspect, is 'responding to experiences, expressing and communicating ideas' (DfES

Learning new things and being adventurous: Jacob and the fountain

2007: 106). A play scenario will describe what this requirement may look like in practice, and this is followed by possible resources that will support the learning and suggestions for aspects of the play that practitioners might observe and note down. Examples of activities and resources from a range of cultural and ethnic backgrounds respond to the EYFS's requirement to be inclusive in supporting all children's creativity. Examples come from established good practice and aim to help practitioners provide a rich environment for children and to extend their own understanding. Each of the four aspects of creativity in the EYFS will be examined in this way, across the full age range from birth to the end of the foundation stage. This part of the book provides a straightforward and essentially practical guide to supporting children in their journey towards achieving this early learning goal.

Each of the activities is preceded by one or more of the requirements in the Development matters column as stated in the EYFS. These are specific to the activity concerned. It is important to note that there are other Development matters requirements that do not specifically refer to the chosen scenario. These are clearly set out in the guidance, and practitioners need to make constant reference to them.

Alongside the practical sections of the book this chapter provides the theoretical framework that underpins all the suggestions and ideas described in Chapters 1–4. A good understanding of why and how teaching and learning happens in particular ways in the early years is critical to its successful implementation. For example, early years practitioners need to know why play is the key to young children's successful learning before they can confidently set up a learning environment that engages children's individual curiosity and promotes creativity. There will be the opportunity for practitioners to question and reflect on their practice in the light of the theories discussed. In recognising the central part that creativity plays in our lives, this book aims to celebrate those aspects which we all have, to a greater or lesser extent: questioning, originality and imagination.

A theoretical base

A definition of creativity

Creativity is one of those concepts that everybody uses; they think they know what it is but, when challenged, find it almost impossible to define. Wikipedia lists more than sixty definitions in psychological literature alone, and that is without the literary and educational ones. However, creativity can be usefully thought of as the ability to construct something new out of things or ideas that already exist. Imagination is an integral part of that process as it is crucial in picturing what doesn't yet exist. The Government's own document *All Our Futures* has this suggestion of a definition: 'Creativity is an imaginative activity fashioned so as to produce outcomes that are both original and of value' (NACCE 1999: 29).

Here is an example. Jo is a young child at the creative area in an early years setting. He is nearly five years old. The setting he attends is well organised and richly resourced with easy-to-find boxes, paper, glue, scissors, a stapler and hole punch. Andy, an early years practitioner, is nearby keeping an eye on proceedings. Jo stands in front of the selection of materials and tools, and, in his imagination, pictures the car he would like to make. What happens next is quite astonishing. He matches his picture of the car to the materials and tools in front of him and makes the decision that he can create his imagined car from the resources that he can see. Next, he selects what he knows he will need by constantly matching his imagined picture to the resources. He begins to create his car by choosing a square box and finding four cardboard discs to make the wheels. His progress from here on is dependent on a number of crucial factors, for example how much practice he has had at imagining and creating, his manual dexterity, his level of confidence and his ability to seek help.

All goes well for a while as he sticks the wheels to each corner of his car. But then disaster strikes as he gets impatient waiting for the glue to dry and tries to help the process along a bit by adding some Sellotape to the joins. The wet, sticky muddle that follows is nearly enough to daunt him, but he sees Andy, the practitioner, nearby and says, 'I can't do this.'

'Which bit do you need help with?' asks Andy, eager to help but not wanting to take over.

'I can't get the wheels to stick on', says Jo. From then onwards, a careful sharing of skills and ideas enables new discs to be stapled on to the corners of the car and a hole to be cut in the roof so that Jo can put some toy passengers inside. Andy's knowledge of Jo's level of development helps him decide that Jo is happy with his car as it now is and considers it finished. Jo is not yet at the stage of wanting to decorate it or to make the wheels turn. Jo rushes to the road-map mat on the floor and joins several of his friends who are playing with toy cars, lorries and buses.

These are the important parts of this scene that have helped Jo to create his car:

- The setting is well resourced with equipment that is likely to stimulate Jo's curiosity.

- There are adults who understand what the potential learning is from the creativity area.

- The adults know Jo well enough to realise what he is most likely to need help with and at what point he will be satisfied with his model.

- Jo has enough trust in Andy and enough self-confidence to ask for help.

- There is enough time for Jo to try out his ideas, make mistakes and, finally, to succeed.

The process that Jo has been through was referred to above as astonishing, and so it is in terms of the complexity of thought needed to turn an idea into a creation that is finished and can be used. Everyone goes through this process, whether they are an artist facing a blank canvas or a mother making up a story to soothe a tired toddler. The application of an idea to make something new is at the heart of creativity. The process may be complex (like the artist's) or simple (like the mother's) but each is purposeful, satisfying and unique.

The EYFS themes and commitments card reinforces what has been suggested above: 'When children have opportunities to play with ideas in different situations and with a variety of resources, they discover connections and come to new and better understandings and ways of doing things. Adult support in this critical process enhances their ability to think critically and ask questions' (DfES 2007: Card 4.3).

The five conditions for creativity

Let us look at each of the five conditions that helped Jo create his model and examine the theory behind each one in order to better understand why they were necessary to Jo's success.

1. The setting is well resourced with equipment that is likely to stimulate Jo's curiosity. Research tells us that development of the brain depends not only on the genes we are born with but also on the experiences we have. This is sometimes called the 'Nature versus Nurture' debate. The development of magnetic resonance scanners has enabled us to see just what happens inside babies' and young children's brains. The scanner shows brain activity in the parts of the brain which can be seen to light up when there is something that interests them and arouses their curiosity. It is this curiosity that is the motivating force that keeps them struggling with a problem or spending a long time getting things 'just right' (Shore 1997). We also know that experiences children have will impact on their later life and will affect who they become as adults (Ball 1994). Children's brains work twice as fast as those of adults, trying to make sense of and understand the world around them. We need, as practitioners, to make sure that the resources we provide for them to use in our settings are of the highest quality so that we create an environment where ideas will be nurtured and thus children will then have the confidence to use their ideas to 'make creations'. This is what is meant by the EYFS theme 'enabling environments'. When thinking about resources, it is important to recognise that 'good quality' does not necessarily mean expensive. What is meant here is that they are 'fit for purpose', for example, that pencils are sharp and that boxes are carefully sorted for ease of selection and their contents not tipped together in an untidy heap. It is hard to be creative when you can't see the materials you need or when the tools you need to use are not in good condition. The other important aspect to resources is how children are allowed to use them. Research carried out in 2000 (May 2000) showed that if children were allowed to use resources in different parts of the setting (for example, if the bricks were taken into the outdoor sand), and that they were able to use them in a variety of ways of the children's choosing, the complexity of their play was increased and their conversations were more involved.

2. There are adults who understand what the potential learning is from the creativity area. At the heart of Jo's endeavours to build his car has been the knowledge that he does not have to achieve this very complex task alone. When he starts to construct his car he does not know whether or not he will succeed, but the fact that he has seen what he knows he needs (the right sized and shaped boxes and the discs for the wheels plus the tools he knows from previous experience are to hand) gives him the courage to take the first step and to select his materials.

Andy, as a well-trained and experienced practitioner, knows that creativity is not about pleasing adults or conforming to anyone else's ideas. As the EYFS practice guidance clearly states, 'It is difficult to make creative connections in learning when colouring in a worksheet or making a Diwali card just like everyone else's' (DfES 2007: card 4.3).

So, Andy is prepared to follow Jo's lead and to be involved, or not, depending on whether he is invited by Jo to help. The ethos of Andy's setting is one where the process of creating is considered much more important than the end product, and what is important to him is the effort, concentration and struggle that Jo is prepared to commit to his task. Children will often spend a very long time creating something that may not 'be' anything; they may be practising their ability to use scissors, glue and Sellotape. They are still, however, involved in the creative process, and Andy knows better than to ever ask the question 'What are you making?' Much more helpful to the young creator are questions about the *process* of the creation such as 'Which bits did you join up first?' or 'How did you decide what needed to go on the top?' These types of questions are ones that children can realistically answer, and they also help them to reflect on what they have done and to use language to describe and discuss their work. These are skills that are going to be increasingly necessary as they become more experienced and discriminating and develop their creative abilities.

3. The adults know Jo well enough to realise what he is most likely to need help with and at what point he will be satisfied with his model. The fact that Andy, whom he knows well and who has helped him in the past, is standing nearby, adds to Jo's confidence that this creation may be achievable. Research in 2003 found that in all effective early years settings the key factor in the children's learning was 'sustained shared thinking', that is, where 'two or more individuals work together in an intellectual way to solve a problem, clarify a concept, evaluate an activity, extend a narrative etc.' (Sylva et al. 2003). This is exactly what Jo and Andy do when Jo finds that he cannot manage the sticky situation he finds himself in when trying to get his car wheels to stay in place. Before Andy can engage in 'sustained shared thinking' with Jo, he needs to know for himself what the possibilities are. He also needs to know what level of development Jo has reached so that he can offer help at just the right moment. He needs to know what can be achieved at this creativity area; that there is the right equipment and that there is enough time for him and Jo to spend long enough to get a satisfactory result. This has implications for planning and timetabling as Andy will need to know that he will not have to be in another area of the setting for a while and that he can spend time talking with Jo to negotiate alternatives to help solve his problems.

The most effective point at which adults intervene in children's learning is often known as 'the zone of proximal development'. Lev Vygotsky, a Russian theorist, described what children could do without any help as their 'zone of *actual* development' and what they can only do with some help as their 'zone of *proximal* development' (Vygotsky 1978). The zone of proximal development is what they can almost do but will not achieve without the help of someone more experienced who knows them well and who is interested in their learning progress. Andy joins Jo in his zone of proximal development as he struggles with the wheels of his car but is very careful not to take away the ownership of the project from Jo. He asks him open-ended questions such as 'Which bit do you need help with?', 'Have you thought of trying it this way?' and 'Would you like to try some new wheels?' All the way through this conversation, Jo remains in control, with Andy in the supporting role, making suggestions and enabling Jo to succeed. 'Sustained shared thinking' means a genuine sharing of ideas. Each of those words is important. The project must be genuinely *shared* between the two participants and the conversation must be *sustained* so that a deep level of *thinking* can take place.

4. Jo has enough trust in Andy and enough self-confidence to ask for help. This key aspect of successful creative learning also considers the relationship between Jo and Andy but concentrates rather more on the trust that Jo has in Andy and the self-confidence that Jo has rather than Andy's professional knowledge.

We know from research that these feelings of trust and self-confidence are crucial in children's ability to succeed. Carol Dweck, in her research into different learning styles, found that children's views of themselves as either 'mastery' or 'helpless' learners had a huge impact on how they tackled a task, particularly a creative one which has no predictable outcome and no guarantee of success (Dweck 1998). How will Jo feel if he fails in his endeavours to make a car? Is he self-confident enough to risk failure or will the experience of failing reinforce his view of himself as a 'helpless' style of learner? Of course, young children do not consciously think through these concepts but they are present nevertheless, and the practitioner can do much to ensure that children come to think of themselves as 'master' learners rather than 'helpless' ones.

Jo clearly does have enough self-confidence to start the unpredictable process of creating his car. His view of himself as someone who is likely to succeed began long before he came to nursery. Since his earliest days he has learnt from the constant interactions with his family: that he is loved, lovable and competent.

All his efforts have been rewarded with interest and praise, and he has already learnt that there are not necessarily only right and wrong answers. There are many ways of trying things out, and, if mistakes are made, they are part of the process of learning. He knows that 'having a go' is an enjoyable challenge and that he will be able to cope if the car-making process turns out to be a struggle. Now that he is at nursery each day, he has found that these views he has about himself and his abilities are shared by the staff who encourage him to try things out even if there is no guarantee of success and will be genuinely interested in and value what he does. This self-confidence is sometimes called a positive disposition to learning.

Alongside this positive attitude of self-confidence, Jo has Andy. Andy is his key person at Nursery and knows him well. The EYFS has recognised that there needs to be a person with special responsibilities to care for each child and that this relationship is an emotional one and not only an administrative one. It may be helpful here to emphasise the distinction between the 'key person' and the 'key worker'. In their book *Key Persons in the Nursery*, Elfer et al. discuss this possible confusion of terms: 'The term "key worker" is used to describe how staff work strategically in nurseries to enhance smooth organisation and record-keeping. This is only one part of being a key person which is an emotional relationship as well as an organisational strategy' (Elfer et al. 2003: 19). It is the *emotional* part of Andy's relationship with Jo that gives Jo the confidence to embark on something which is untried and could go very wrong.

Jo is secure in the knowledge that Andy cares for him, will be interested in his model and will offer help if it is needed. The EYFS says that 'Babies and children become independent by being able to depend upon adults for reassurance and comfort' (DfES 2007: Card 4.3). Certainly, in the uncertain world of creating new things, independence of thought and ideas is at the centre of the process, and, for that to happen, children need someone nearby on whom they can depend.

5. There is enough time for Jo to try out his ideas, make mistakes and, finally, to succeed. In her book *Listening to Four Year Olds*, Jacqui Cousins noted that one of children's most hated aspects of nursery life was being interrupted in the middle of an enthralling activity: 'When such an interruption occurred, I observed how seldom children were able to pick up the threads of their thinking or their action' (Cousins 1999: 36). Not only is there genuine irritation at being stopped before a project is complete, but the project itself is rarely revived, and the creative thoughts and ideas are lost. This has serious implications for children's desire to keep trying to be creative as they learn that one of the key factors they need, that of time, is not available to them in sufficient quantity. If this is a constant pattern of nursery life, learning becomes less deep, thought becomes less complex, and creativity becomes less of a possibility.

Why creativity is important

At the beginning of this chapter it was suggested that creativity is one of the fundamental building blocks of human beings. If we, as practitioners, are to be true educators, we must enable all the children in our care to be able to think critically, to act creatively and to be confident in the use of their imagination.

All societies need a population who can imagine and think in innovative and creative ways. These people will not only run large institutions and make new scientific discoveries but will also raise the next generation with thoughtfulness and insight and have the adaptability to survive the significant changes that lie ahead. Societies in the past that have declined have been those who have become complacent and have lost the ability or the disposition to think critically, to imagine alternatives and to apply them.

In the town of Reggio Emilia, in northern Italy, an entire early years culture has been founded on just this idea. When deciding what kind of early years schooling the community in Reggio Emilia wanted to create, the response was one founded on their experiences under the rule of Mussolini in the Second World War. The Mayor of Reggio Emilia in the 1960s stated that 'the fascist experience had taught them that people who conformed and obeyed were dangerous and that in building a new society it was imperative to safeguard and communicate that lesson and nurture and maintain a vision of children who can think and act for themselves' (Dahlberg 1995: 12).

It may seem rather extreme to bring politics into the world of early years but, as we are currently experiencing in our own country, the kind of education we give our very young children is often a political 'hot potato'. All institutions, be they schools, industries or hospitals, are more straightforward to manage, evaluate and fund if the customers and workforce are obedient, compliant and, therefore, predictable. Current and recent UK governments have increasingly required schools, and now childcare settings, to meet targets which are matched to financial support. This requires schools and settings to conform to a 'regime of performability' with practitioners 'trained as technicians within a competence-based training' (Petri 2005: 293). The result of this trend to performance-based education is reported almost daily in the press as anxieties are expressed about our society's 'loss of childhood'. A UNICEF report in 2007 stated that UK children were the least happy in Europe, and a new organisation called 'Open Eye' reflects many practitioners' concerns that government interventions in early education may place too much external pressure on settings to emphasise target-setting and formal assessment over creativity and play. The worry is that with too formal an approach in the nursery, the conditions that helped Jo to create his car in the example above will be harder for practitioners to preserve.

The stages of creativity

The creative process is complex. It consists of several stages which may all take a considerable length of time.

- First, the environment around young children must be stimulating so that curiosity is aroused and the desire to discover is developed. This is sometimes known as the *disposition,* to investigate what is seen, heard, touched and felt. The question inside children's heads at this stage may be thought of as 'What is it?'

- The next stage could be called the *incubation* or the *simmering*. At this stage, children explore and play with the materials that have intrigued them, and the question inside their heads could be described as 'What does it do and what can I do with it?'

- Finally comes the *hatching* part of the process which involves the children taking control of both the materials they have been exploring and the ideas they have attached to them. The question now in children's heads can be thought of as 'What can I create using these things?'

As Bernadette Duffy suggests, 'These levels overlap and evolve out of each other. The process may take place over a period of a few hours or over many days' (1998: 81). It is certainly a process that cannot be rushed.

The environment around the young child must be stimulating:
a picture of the London Eye after a visit

As we saw with Jo and his car, time is needed to make mistakes. No one can create something new if they are unfamiliar with the materials to be used. Jo will have already spent a lot of time exploring and practising with the scissors, card, glue and Sellotape before having enough confidence in his abilities to start making his car. He will also have spent some considerable time mulling over his ideas. This is sometimes called 'down time' and is a vital element of creativity. Many of the best-known 'eureka' moments, such as Newton's discovery of gravity and Archimedes' understanding of displacement theory, happen when the creator or discoverer is not currently thinking about what is about to be discovered. The ideas of gravity and displacement had clearly been incubating for a long while in Newton's and Archimedes' minds, until, at a quite unexpected moment of relaxation under the apple tree or in the bath, the light dawned and a new theory was understood for the first time.

In the current educational climate, it is important to protect children's opportunity for down time so that they have time to watch, reflect and incubate ideas. However, it is sometimes difficult for practitioners to justify time when children do not appear to be busy, and too often it is thought that the contemplative child is wasting time or being lazy. A small group time each day, where children are encouraged to reflect on their ideas and creations and listen to other's ideas and points of view can help to slacken the pace just enough to allow for some nurturing of creative ideas.

The spiral curriculum

Jerome Bruner talked about these stages of understanding as being a 'spiral curriculum'. He suggested that children will return to play activities time and time again, bringing with them ever more experience, competence and maturity. Each time children revisit an activity their understanding will have increased, their play will be more complex and their ideas more involved. This has huge implication for us as practitioners, because if we are continually changing the setting's provision children do not have a chance to come back to a play activity to deepen their knowledge and develop their skills. The time that Jo has already spent at the creative area mulling and incubating his ideas is the perfect preparation for the experience of producing a creation.

Creativity and play

The government document *All Our Futures* states that creative processes require 'freedom and control; the freedom to experiment and the control of skills, knowledge and understandings' (DfES 1999: 38). The tension between freedom elements and control elements of creativity is one that needs exploring as there is often some concern amongst practitioners that when children are being creative they are more likely to be troublesome and disobedient. 'It is important to remember that we are not talking about uninhibited self-expression. The creative process is about intellectual freedom to explore ideas, not the freedom to do what you want' (Duffy 1998). The more control that adults try to impose on children's ideas, the less opportunity there will be for creativity in the setting. The practitioner must recognise this and make a professional decision as to what the balance of control will be to allow imagination and creativity to flourish.

Practitioners have complete control of many aspects of their setting. All the resources – that is, equipment, time and adults' roles – are managed and organised by them. The ethos and culture (including the expectations of children and adults) are in the control of the lead practitioner as is most of the process of planning and assessment, though these last two can often be a very successful shared venture. What is left for children to control is the use of resources. In most settings, the use of resources is divided between adult-initiated use and child-initiated use, the latter we call 'play'. It is clear, therefore, that the adults have a large measure of control but that they must leave the ownership of children's ideas to the children; they won't be short of them!

Key aspects of play

Play is a process that is intensely creative, and, because of that, it lies at the heart of effective practice in the early years setting. Play has the following elements that make it ideal as a creative process:

1   It is an active process without necessarily an end product.
2   It is intrinsically motivated.
3   It is about possible, alternative worlds which involve 'supposing' and 'as if' which lifts players to their highest levels of functioning. This involves being imaginative, creative, original and innovative.
4   It is an integrating mechanism which brings together everything we know, feel and can do.

(Bruce 1991)

All of the above aspects of play are both observable by the trained practitioner and underlined by research and educational theory.

Play is an active process without necessarily an end product.   The theories of Jean Piaget (1896–1980) were characterised by notions of active learning and first-hand experience. He described children as being like 'lone scientists' (Piaget 1973), each one making his or her own discoveries about how the world works based on their developmental level and experiences. This was revolutionary at the time as most teaching was based on the 'transmission' model with children learning facts by rote. Although many of Piaget's ideas have been challenged and developed, his influence on the pedagogy of early years practice cannot be overstated as it was he who gave us the concept of exploratory learning by first-hand experience. He believed that it is through children's play that they use what they already know to bring understanding to their current experiences. Piaget called the child's knowledge about a concept a *schema* and suggested that constant practice of these schemas enabled children to securely embed a concept in the brain. We can all recall children in our settings who seem to play compulsively with one activity for many days or weeks at a time, making secure their understanding about how things get, for example, from one place to another (transporting schema) – or children who spend a large part of each day joining long sections of the Brio train track together as they explore the joining schema. Play provides an excellent way for children to try out new concepts that they need to learn about and to practise them in different contexts.

Lev Vygotsky (1896–1934) and Jerome Bruner (b. 1915) both emphasised the social nature of the learning process and built on Piaget's theories of first-hand exploratory learning by suggesting the crucial role that a more expert companion has in furthering children's understandings. You will remember that Vygotsky named the point at which adults can most usefully help children to learn something new as the zone of proximal development. Bruner talks of the process of adults helping children to learn as 'scaffolding' (Woods et al. 1976). In the same way as scaffolding supports a building under construction, practitioners' suggestions support children's learning. Both Vygotsky and Bruner consider that the roles of the practitioner and of the friend and peer group are of the greatest importance in successfully learning something new. It is this process of learning new concepts and ideas and the need to be able to practise them that is central to creativity as children need to be familiar with the properties of objects and how to use them before they can use them for their own purposes and to create something new with them. Put at its simplest level, Jo would not have attempted to make his car unless he had spent a lot of time previously playing with cardboard, paper, glue, scissors and Sellotape to find out what they could do before attempting anything so complex as making a car. The theory of this model of learning is called 'social constructivist' and is the most effective model of teaching and learning to encourage creativity.

Play is intrinsically motivated. One of the key features of play is that it comes from within and cannot be directed by anyone else. Sometimes the term 'directed play' is used to suggest that adults can have an influence on children's play. However, it is often argued that once play is thought of as 'directed' it is no longer play but falls into the category of adult-directed time. Happily, the EYFS does not use this term but talks of play needing to be 'well planned' and 'based on children's spontaneous play' (DfES 2007: 7). This should help practitioners to ensure that once the well-planned play is set up they can leave the children themselves to maximise the opportunities it offers with confidence.

When planning for purposeful play it is sometimes helpful to consider the difference between 'activities' and 'provision': 'Activities tend, by their nature to be adult planned and led and to have learning objectives and outcomes. Provision, on the other hand, although planned and resourced by the adults, contains a range of learning opportunities with objectives and outcomes that are usually inside the children's minds' (May et al. 2006: 14).

If the majority of what is on offer to children are activities with adult-controlled outcomes, children's opportunities to be creative are much more limited. It is the intrinsic motivation apparent in play that gives children the

Objectives and outcomes are usually inside the children's minds

freedom to try out their own ideas rather than be constrained by adults' intentions. Intrinsic motivation is a great life skill to learn and one of the best motivational forces to aid achievement and success. It is important, therefore, that we constantly review our provision to ensure that the opportunities for play such as role play, small-world play, construction, free drawing, painting, music and model-making are always available, attractively presented and valued so that children will be drawn to these creative opportunities.

Play is about possible, alternative worlds which involve 'supposing' and 'as if' which lifts players to their highest levels of functioning. This involves being imaginative, creative, original and innovative. Research by Ferre Laevers into the quality of children's learning suggested that children who are deeply involved in their learning are likely to be learning effectively. They can be seen to be concentrating, to be energetic and creative, to be persistent and to show precision. They will be articulate and show high levels of satisfaction during their involvement. He described these children as looking like 'fish in water' (Laevers 1994). Children displaying these attributes are often fully engaged in play. It is rather like adults engaged in a hobby. Time passes without being noticed, mistakes are made and problems solved. All is done at a pace that is right for the participant, and there are great feelings of enjoyment and achievement. Whether the adult is gardening, walking, writing a novel, painting a picture or line dancing, the elements of motivation, satisfaction and creativity are common threads that lift the participant to high levels of functioning. For children, play opens up the possibility to function at a higher level as they pretend to drive tractors, make a drink for the baby or visit grandma. The opportunities that play gives children to inhabit other worlds encourages the fostering of one of the keys to creativity, the imagination.

Play is an integrating mechanism that brings together everything we know, feel and can do. During periods of play, children have the freedom to be in charge of their ideas and actions. If we think of Jo and his car, we can see from his level of satisfaction at the end of the project that he felt he had achieved a great deal. It was a project that required him to bring together all he knew about cars and how they worked with all the skills he had developed to manipulate and use the tools. He then brought all his motivation and positive dispositions to the task, and it was the combination of these attributes, together with Andy's help, that led to his eventual success. We can see, then, that to be creative, children need to have a range of abilities. They need to have developed physical skills to be deft enough to make their creation. They need to have enough knowledge about their creation to be clear about what it will look like, and, most important of all, they need to have developed good emotional abilities to persist in the struggle to complete the task. This is why a knowledge of child development is so useful for practitioners as it helps to inform them of children's levels of development and therefore, what they are likely to be able to achieve.

Play, as an integrating mechanism, is also often helpful in a situation where a child has experienced a trauma or a situation that has been worrying

Counting the morning glory flowers: creativity in the wider curriculum

or unfamiliar. In the following chapters we will hear about a child who has recently moved house and one who has been fearful of thunderstorms. Both of these experiences are common in childhood, as are the associated feelings of fear and discontinuity. If they are able to engage in play situations that consider these experiences in a controlled and familiar environment, this will often help children to feel rather more positive about what has happened to them. In the example of making music from the sounds of the thunder and rain, a frightening experience can become the foundation of a genuinely creative one and help the child to see the storm from a different perspective. In the case of moving house, the experience can be practised over and over again with role play. This ensures that children have control of the situation until they feel happier about it. It is important that the play does 'integrate' all children's areas of development. For play will only be effective if children can explore what they feel, what they know and what they can do and bring all of these elements to the play. It is because play is able to offer such integration that it is such a powerful tool for exploring feelings, aims, fears and ideas.

Play, as a process, is not very different from the scene in a scientist's lab where scientists try out their ideas, make mistakes, try something a different way and then have a break for a cup of tea. They talk amongst themselves informally, look something up in book and are unhurried in the journey towards coming to a successful conclusion. This, as a process, is a most helpful way to learn new things, to create and to be innovative – both for scientists and for young children!

Creativity in the wider curriculum

Several aspects of play are very helpful to children when they are learning across the whole EYFS curriculum. Scientists doing experiments are not thought to be 'playing' as such, but the process that they are going through on the way to discovering new things is exactly the same. This same process is also helpful for children learning new skills such as writing and number or when learning new knowledge about the world. Children who are presented with learning in ways that engage their curiosity, whether it be whilst creating a car out of junk or writing their name, will be most likely to be learning at a high level and to be enjoying the process. This helps them to remember what they have learned.

Children who learn in creative ways develop these skills:

- critical thinking (asking questions);
- observation (noticing);
- discussion (talking about what they are learning).

They will also develop these attitudes:

- concentration (spending a long time playing at one activity);
- problem-solving (thinking of different ways to try things);
- patience (being calm and persistent);
- self-confidence (expecting success but accepting failure as part of the learning process);
- enthusiasm (being cheerful and enjoying a challenge).

Practitioners, therefore, need to be imaginative in the ways in which learning is presented to young children across the whole curriculum and not just in that part named 'creativity'. In Chapter 5, for example, we consider the creative ways in which writing is taught in a reception class and note the enthusiasm that was fostered in the children. Creative teaching means just this kind of approach where staff are thoughtful about the skills and attitudes they wish their children to learn and knowledgeable about how to incorporate them into their teaching. These creative skills and attitudes will be valuable throughout the children's lives. The practice guidance makes this point very clear in stating that 'Being creative involves the whole curriculum, not just the arts' (DfES 2007: Card 4.3).

The adults' role in children's creativity

Adults creating a sense of belonging

Humans, as we considered in the introduction to this chapter, have a need to express themselves and to be creative. Abraham Maslow, in his Hierarchy of Needs, suggests that the need to express individuality is at the core of being a fulfilled person but that the conditions must be favourable before self-expression, or 'self-actualisation' as he called it, can take place (Maslow 1943). There are more pressing basic requirements such as the need to be safe, fed and loved that need to be satisfied before most people feel motivated enough to embark on creating and inventing. Most children in our settings are safe and fed, but children also need to know that they are loved, valued and that they feel a part of the community that is their setting before committing themselves to the rather vulnerable business of trying out something new. They need to know that if their creation is not a success, their setting will not think less of them and that they will be encouraged to try again.

A sense of belonging is critical to children's sense of confidence, and adults must ensure that a sensitive companionship surrounds each and every child if a culture of creativity is to thrive.

Adults choosing resources

Effective resources are key to encouraging creativity. Practitioners need to choose resources carefully so that children can use them in a range different of ways, for example the wooden block that can be both a telephone and calculator leads to a much richer imaginative game than toys that have a single function. Resources need to be carefully stored and regularly cleaned so that they are always attractive to use. It is a truism that resources which are well cared for will be played with at a higher level of functioning than those which, it is clear to the children, have little value to the adults. This is particularly noticeable when considering the amount of space to be given to areas such as that for role play. If the role-play area is squashed into a dark corner, and there is not enough equipment, arguments will soon break out between a child who is trying to cook sausages in the same space as someone trying to bath the baby! Poor resourcing gives play a bad name and can worry parents who see that not much learning, creative or otherwise, is taking place in these cramped conditions. They may then begin to press for more formal ways of teaching and learning which appear to be more under the practitioner's control.

Adults helping children to become familiar with materials

Children need a wide range of materials with which to become familiar before they can become innovative and creative. They also need much time and help so that they can learn how to use tools and materials safely and effectively. This is an instance when 'teaching' means just that. Children need clear teaching as to how to use the stapler and scissors, how to play a range of musical instruments and how to do up their paint aprons. When this knowledge is in place and the children have had many opportunities to practise these skills, they are then free to take control of them and to use them as they wish. The practitioner is thus enabling the children to be creative.

Adults being articulate

Both within and beyond the setting, creativity needs to be confidently promoted. More than any other area of the curriculum, its outcomes are uncertain, its process unpredictable and its value often unrecognised. Creativity is not easily measured and is impossible to put into neat learning compartments. Other professionals and families may need convincing that it is necessary for us, in early years settings, to provide an environment that will support children's endeavours to be creative. Part of being an early years specialist is about being able to see the world from inside a child's head and about being able to explain our principles and beliefs to all who need convincing! Often, photographic or videoed evidence of children struggling with their ideas will be enough to demonstrate the high level of function that is involved in making something new, and support for their endeavours will be more widely understood.

Conclusion

Creativity is, then, a complex and a rather slippery concept. Loris Malaguzzi, who founded the infant and toddler schools in Reggio Emilia, suggested that 'Creativity should not be considered a separate mental faculty but a characteristic of our way of thinking, knowing and making choices' (1998a: 79).

Malaguzzi wrote, in his poem 'The Hundred Languages of Children' (1998b) that creative learning is never compartmentalised; it is never about either work or play, either reality or fantasy, either science or imagination. It is the subtle intermingling of these seemingly opposite elements that gives discovering something new its excitement and gives children their many ways of expressing what they have learned. These different ways, as Malaguzzi so powerfully described them, are their 'hundred languages'. We, as early years practitioners, must protect these 'languages' so that the children in our care can use their many different ways of expressing and thus become creative learners.

Being creative

From birth–11 months

> ### Development matters
>
> - Responding to experiences.
>
> - Expressing and communicating ideas.
>
> - Using movement and sensory exploration to connect with their immediate environment.
>
> ### Key words
> security, prediction

Activity

Julia is seven months old. She has been with her childminder Sue for a few weeks as her mother returned to work after taking maternity leave. Sue is using lots of ways to get to know Julia really well and to help Julia feel safe and loved in her new setting. Singing with her is one of the very best ways of building this important friendship, and Sue sings nursery rhymes and songs every day.

Sue picks Julia up and stands her on her lap so that they are face to face. 'Shall we sing a song?' says Sue. Sue begins to sing the 'Ready and …' song which Julia has heard a few times before:

Ready and …
Up and down
And up and down
And side to side
And side to side.
Round and round
And round and round
And ready to do it again …
Ready and …
(PEEP 2001: 20)

Sue gently lifts Julia up and down, from side to side and round and round as she sings the song, and, by the third time she sings 'Ready and …', Julia's eyes get wider, and her toes kick down on to Sue's lap as she excitedly waits to be lifted up and down.

Learning story

- **Emotional learning.** For babies to be able to respond to an environment, the environment has to be both interesting and loving. For babies, all their learning comes via someone else so the key to their successful learning is that they feel loved by their carer. This kind of interaction with babies is often called 'mother-ese' because it is how mothers instinctively behave with their babies. It is a powerful means of communication because Julia is learning so many things from this most natural of activities. She is learning that Sue enjoys being with her and that she is, therefore, a lovable person. (See 'key person', p. 7.)

- **Social learning.** Julia is learning that Sue is someone she can trust and someone who will both care for her and be her partner in enjoyable activities.

- **Cognitive learning.** Julia is learning some basis concepts here about directions. The way that we all learn about what it means to be 'up', 'down' and 'round' is to experience them at first hand. She is also learning to predict what will happen next and that things often happen in a predictable order.

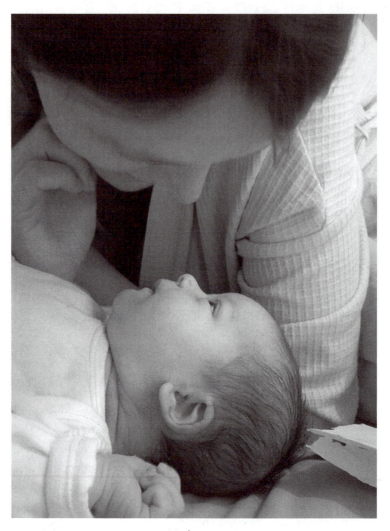

Motherese

 Look, listen and note

- It is essential to watch babies' body language to better understand their individual preferences and dislikes.

- Observe them carefully to ensure that they feel safe and loved and note aspects of their emotional well-being as well as taking care of their physical needs.

Effective practice

- This includes valuing and respecting babies' preferences once they have been observed.

- Practitioners need to demonstrate that they enjoy the baby's company and find time and a comfortable space to share these valuable experiences together.

- Practitioners will, of course need to go through this process with each of their key children.

Planning

Singing with young babies needs to be planned into every session as it is a key way to build the loving relationship that babies need. It needs to be planned as a one-to-one activity, somewhere it is quiet, and where there is a big comfortable chair or sofa, where there is room to do actions.

Resourcing

PEEP has a wealth of video and of other support materials for parents and carers for birth to four years. Look out for nursery-rhyme books such as *The Helen Oxenbury Collection* or *The Oxford Nursery Rhyme Book* by Iona Opie and Peter Opie.

The EYFS principles

The four principles of the EYFS are also to be seen in this simple example. Sue may well have tried a few songs before finding this one, which Julia clearly loves. For a carer to understand that each child is unique it requires them to be responsive to individual children's preferences, and even very small babies can tell you which songs they like the best! It is a sign of the positive relationship between Sue and Julia that Sue takes time to find out which Julia's favourites are and that she respects these choices. She will also have introduced her to other songs and rhymes, but a sign of her responsiveness as a carer is that she knows which ones are Julia's favourites and that she makes a point of singing them regularly.

The environment in which this kind of activity takes place is an important factor. Songs between two people who are building a strong and loving relationship need to take place where they can be quiet and can concentrate. They need to be comfortable and to be at a time in the day when Julia is not tired or hungry.

From 8–20 months

Development matters

- Respond to what they see, hear, smell, touch and feel.

Key words
investigate, enjoyment

Activity

Josh is twelve months old and has been at his nursery setting for four months. He attends for three days a week from 8 a.m. till 6 p.m. His key person Ali has noticed how much his face lights up when he hears music. She places him in a group of other children about his age and brings the treasure basket from which they can choose something to examine and play with. Josh chooses a small plastic bottle which has water inside and some shiny beads and buttons, securely fastened at the lid with tape. As he grasps the shaker and begins to shake it to and fro he looks at Ali who responds by clapping her hands in time to his actions and smiling at his enthusiastic waving.

Josh is able to respond to what is around him, first because there are colourful and interesting things for him to investigate and second because he has a key worker who has got to know him well and understands what is likely to engage his interest.

Learning story

- **Emotional learning.** Josh is learning that he is someone who is valued and liked and that people enjoy spending time in his company and think it is important to find out what interests him. (See 'key person', p. 7.)

- **Social learning.** Josh is finding out that nursery is a place where there are many things to arouse his curiosity. Children come 'hard-wired' to learn about how the world works, and a rich environment will be a key factor in engaging Josh's imagination. (See 'rich environment', p. 7.)

- **Cognitive learning.** Josh is learning about what happens when he waves the bottle to and fro and that he is in control of the movement. With practice he will understand about cause and effect and that he can create rhythms with his actions.

Look, listen and note

- The skill here is to observe babies to learn what attracts their attention and watch them carefully as they make their choices.

- Note what these choices are and link them into the setting's planning to ensure that they are available.

Effective practice

Ensure that materials are available to babies which will encourage them to try out new and favourite activities. These materials should be in good condition, easily available and attractive. Some should be made of natural materials.

Planning

The treasure basket needs thoughtful preparation. It needs to be of wicker or strong cardboard, around 350 millimetres across and 120 millimetres high. It should be strong enough not to be tipped over when placed on a rug, and the material it contains should be a mixture of natural and manufactured items – but not conventional plastic toys. The items should be interesting to look at, to touch, listen to and feel.

Resourcing

Things to collect or make

- pine cones
- ribbons, lace or velvet
- large shells
- plastic bottles containing beads or buttons
- woollen pom-poms
- tubes from inside kitchen roll
- egg cups
- lavender bags.

Things to buy

- little bells
- napkin ring
- spoons
- a lemon

- a little rag doll or other figures, including animals

- shiny wrapping paper.

The list is endless!

The EYFS principles

The four principles of the EYFS can also clearly be seen in this activity as Ali has recognised the uniqueness of Josh by thinking about his enjoyment of music and catering for that interest. The rich environment supports a wide range of children's interests and provides musical instruments from several cultures which children can bang and shake. (See 'rich environment', p. 7.) Ali Ⓒ is responsive to Josh as she enables him to engage in an activity that gives him particular enjoyment, thus reinforcing his understanding that his relationship with her is positive and strong.

From 16–26 months

Development matters

- Express themselves through physical action and sound.

Key words
challenge, developing competence

Activity

At twenty months, Mari is now a competent walker. She has been watching children at her nursery climb the five steps to the top of the slide and their obvious delight as they come down the slippery slope shouting 'Wheeee!' Farah, her key person, suspects that Mari will now be able to use the slide herself but is possibly lacking the self-confidence to try it out.

'Would you like to try climbing, Mari?' asks Farah.

Mari nods and walks to the bottom of the steps where she pauses uncertainly and looks round for Farah.

'It's alright, Mari, I'm here,' says Farah.

She stands immediately behind Mari and encourages her to put a foot on the bottom step. Very slowly and carefully Mari makes her way up the steps with Farah just behind her all the way. At the top, Mari spends around ten minutes looking around, sitting down and then standing up again. When she is feeling safe at the top, Farah says, 'Tell you what, Mari, I'll be at the bottom of the slide for when you want to come down, would that be good?'

Mari sits down at the top of the slide and nods. Farah goes round to the bottom of the slide and stands with a big smile on her face and her arms stretched out. After what seems like a long while, Mari pushes herself on to the slippery slope and down into Farah's waiting arms.

'Wow!', says Farah, 'what a clever girl, do you want to do that again?'

Another nod from Mari, and the two of them make their way back to the foot of the slide.

A key feature of this example is that very young children need to respond to the physical environment and to express themselves physically even if there is some, assessed, risk attached. Physical achievement is always enjoyed by young children who, when they say to a practitioner, 'Look what I can do!' are usually referring to a physical challenge that they have over-come. It may be tempting to ensure that children as young as Mari are always kept safely at ground level but we know that 'Attention, balance and co-ordination are the primary ABC on which all later learning depends' (Blythe 2000). These gross motor skills that Mari is beginning to develop will also help her later on when she needs to develop the small motor skills that she will need to draw, to write and to paint.

Learning story

- **Emotional learning.** Mari could not achieve this huge challenge without the support of her key person. The trust that she has in Farah gives her the courage to try something right on the edge of her ability, and the belief that Farah shows in her helps her to believe in herself as a learner. 'I think I can do this' is her unspoken attitude to the challenge, and the success will raise her confidence levels still higher. (See 'mastery learner', p. 9.)

- **Social learning.** Mari has gained from watching the other children using the slide. Watching and taking an interest are vital starting points for children who are curious but not yet quite at the stage of being able to try out an activity for themselves. It is important not to hurry children along too quickly as the watching stage is the one where children are matching their interests and abilities to the experience on offer and asking themselves, 'Is this something I would like to do?'

- **Cognitive learning.** Mari, perhaps for the first time, is seeing her familiar toys, nursery garden and friends from a different perspective – from above. As a result, she is likely to become very interested in the concepts of 'up' and 'down' and to enjoy songs such as 'The Grand Old Duke of York', especially if it is accompanied by 'up and down' actions. She may begin to use the words 'up' and 'down' when she sits down and stands up and to notice birds and aeroplanes high in the sky as she considers related concepts and words such as 'high' and 'low'. She learns, as well, that going up, or climbing, is an effort that requires hard work whereas coming down is fast and exciting. These two experiences feel very different and may well help Mari begin to experience the concept of gravity. (See 'schemas', p. 16.)

Look, listen and note

Farah needs to have observed Mari regularly to be able to assess her physical capabilities and then to match these capabilities to the equipment in the setting. This accurate matching enables Mari to experience success in what is, for her, a challenging activity.

Effective practice

- A risk assessment is necessary with equipment that presents children with a physical challenge. Farah needs to know that the equipment has been checked for safety and that Mari will be able to use it at her own pace, without other children crowding her.

- Time will need to be allowed for Mari to consider her actions and to build up enough confidence to use the slide with success.

Planning

Equipment that helps children's gross motor skills to develop needs stringent monitoring for safety. At the start of each session, practitioners must check that all locking and safety bolts and latches are in position and that all equipment will be adequately staffed. During long spells of wet weather, consider opportunities for children to climb, crawl, balance and jump indoors.

Resourcing

- Large climbing structures with poles, platforms, slides, bridges, ladders and steps.

- Barrels and soft play equipment.

- Tricycles.

- Games equipment such as balls and large skittles.

- Building blocks and balancing beams.

The EYFS principles

The four principles of the EYFS are present here too. Mari's key person has observed her closely and knows that although Mari is a small child physically, she is curious about new situations and is often keen to try out new things. She has also noticed that Mari particularly enjoys physical activities and has used the tunnel in the nursery garden to crawl through many times. She has a good sense of balance and good gross motor skills, and it was this professional knowledge that Farah used when deciding that Mari would probably be able to use the slide. Mari has a unique set of talents and skills, and Farah, as her key person, knows her well and can therefore make decisions about her learning that are based on fact and likely to lead to success. (See 'key person', p. 25.)

The environment of this nursery garden has been set up thoughtfully by the nursery staff to enable just such challenges to happen. They have talked through the fact that the slide presents risks but these are minimised by ensuring that a qualified member of staff is always in attendance. The slide is an everyday piece of equipment so that children have regular opportunities to use it and to become proficient. It is this well-considered planning that enables children to use challenging equipment safely and competently.

The positive relationship that Mari and Farah enjoy is clearly a key feature of Mari's successful learning. We know that by 'scaffolding' a new piece of learning, a child's important person whom they trust can help them achieve much more than they could do on their own. This relationship is seen to be responsive as Farah follows Mari's interests and also to be sensitive as she offers exactly the level of support that Mari needs to be courageous enough to climb the slide. (See 'scaffolding', p. 16.)

From 22–36 months

Development matters

- Explore by repeating patterns of play.

Key words

transporting schema, reaching new understandings

Activity

In the day-care setting that Val and her friend Suzy attend there is a well-stocked role-play area. The friends are both just over two years old. At the moment, the role-play area is set up to be used as a café, with tables, chairs, plates, tablecloths, cutlery and menu cards for children to choose what they would like to order. Each day recently, Val and Suzy have come to play in the café, bringing with them their dolls and buggies. To the practitioners' dismay, they have packed up the entire contents of the café into their buggies and wheeled them to the book area where they have carefully unpacked all the café equipment and have laid out the tablecloth and cutlery on the carpet in the book area. Then they have invited friends to come and look at the menu cards and choose what they would like to eat.

The café is, in effect, relocated to the book area each session that Val and Suzy attend the setting, and no amount of gentle questioning by the practitioners has elicited an answer from the two children about their actions. Their reply to questioning each session is 'We'll put it all back when we've finished', which they always do!

However, as this repeated action means that none of the other children in the setting can use the role-play area as the practitioners had intended, it is decided that Val's and Suzy's actions must be observed and a decision made by staff as to how to approach this apparently inflexible use of equipment.

In one of the books in the staff area there is a chapter about children's repeated patterns of play, and the manager reads this section with her staff at a planning meeting. The staff recognise Val's and Suzy's play as a 'schema' where the children almost compulsively play to learn about how things are transported from one place to another. (See 'schema', p. 16.)

The book suggests ways in which staff can support children who are exploring different concepts through schematic play. One of the other members of staff remembers that there are two other children who regularly build the wooden train track across the entire setting floor and that she cannot recall a train ever being played with on the track! She thinks that perhaps these children are learning about how things join together through a 'connecting' schema. The setting manager then remembers that Suzy's family has just moved house and perhaps that is the reason that the concept of transporting is so important to her. The staff suggest reading *Teddy Bear's Moving Day* to Suzy's group the next day to further help Suzy become comfortable with ideas about moving.

They have invited friends

A key feature of this example of creative play is the sensitivity and responsiveness of the staff. On realising that Suzy had important learning needs by playing in the way that she was, staff were eager to support her as best they could. By allowing Suzy to explore her feelings and ideas, they were making a significant contribution to her progress. They then thought of other resources, such as books, that they could use to help her explore and express her ideas about moving house.

Learning story

- **Emotional learning.** Suzy has experienced big changes in her life by moving house. So many things that were important to her, like her bedroom, her friends and her routine of going to her nursery have changed, and very young children find change one of the most difficult situations to deal with emotionally. To be able to play at transporting things from one place to another with her closest friend helps her begin to feel rather more in control of what has happened to her. When playing, children are always in control of the game, and this feeling gives them a sense of autonomy and self-confidence. Suzy can create a range of different games about moving, such as getting lost, leaving something behind or finding new places for the dolls and books which will help her explore some of the challenges of moving but in a safe way with a friend she trusts.

- **Social learning.** The early years setting is an excellent place for children to explore and express feelings and ideas, especially those that unsettle them. Suzy has found a good friend in Val, who is happy to play with her and who may have her own reasons for wanting to play at 'moving house'. There may well be changes in her life, too, or it may be that playing with a 'special' friend each day gives her confidence and a sense of continuity. All children will have their own 'agenda', their own reason for wanting to be involved in the game. Val's reasons may not be the same as Suzy's, but the companionship is important for her and provides an opportunity for them both to learn about the 'give and take' of genuine friendship.

- **Cognitive learning.** When children are involved in schematic play, they have the opportunity to become progressively more sure about the concept they are interested in. As Suzy keeps repeating her transporting schema, it is as if she is practising her thoughts and ideas about moving. Through this play these ideas become clearer to her. She becomes more settled, and the moving game comes to a natural end. Cathy Nutbrown calls learning in this way 'Patterns of play with threads of thinking running through them' (1994). Bernadette Duffy says that 'When children are engaged in a schema, they are engaged in a creative process, as they are making new connections and reaching new understandings' (1998: 84). It is important to support children in this type of play because children are enabled, first to learn about new things and second to make the learning meaningful for them in their unique situation.

Look, listen and note

- Any repeated, rather compulsive, play patterns that children show should be observed and notes made to share information with the other adults at planning meetings.

- Note children's schematic behaviour in their records with the date and consider sharing this information with families.

Effective practice

- Having noted and planned to support children's schematic play; equipment, materials and time should be made readily available for children to follow their preferred patterns of play.

- Ways for children to extend their schematic play by other activities or using other material should be offered.

- Refer to textbooks, magazines and other experts to help explain unusual behaviour.

Planning

Planning needs to be responsive, with practitioners noticing a child's compulsive play patterns. Discussions with staff can help all adults to make suggestions as to how to support this play.

Resourcing

- As schemas are all-embracing, children need a wide range of materials to explore them. This can be done using small-world play with train sets, model farms and other set pieces. Role play could also be used, as well as construction toys and painting and creative materials.

- A good stock of children's books in a setting is obvious. However, it is also beneficial to build a library of adult books on the theory and good practice of early years education to supplement the directives.

- Gretz, Susanna (1981) *Teddy Bear's Moving Day,* London: Ernest Benn.

The EYFS principles

The EYFS principles are evident in this piece of play. Suzy's unique needs have been observed and noted by the well-trained staff, and actions put in place to support her further. Staff have also considered Val's needs by ensuring that this regular play continues to be useful for her too. The practitioners have gained an insight into repeated play patterns that children engage in and will be more aware of them in the future.

The fact that the staff are both sensitive to and responsive to children's needs helps them to view schematic play as a powerful tool that children can use to learn new concepts and not as a nuisance when the equipment is used in different ways from those which had been intended. The close links with children's families give staff valuable knowledge about what is happening in children's lives, and the trust that Suzy's family have in the practitioners means that a helpful conversation can take place as staff and parents talk through Suzy's current learning and emotional needs.

The sensitive attitude of this setting means that staff are aware of children's needs and adapt their planning accordingly. This results in an environment where Suzy is helped to develop her interest in moving and where she can be confident that she can continue to learn about what is important for her.

From 22–36 months

Development matters

- Seek to make sense of what they see, hear, touch and feel.

Key words

heightening awareness of the senses, companionable learning

Activity

Carl is nearly three. He has a childminder, Jan, who he is with for three days a week. There is often a baby in the house who Jan cares for as well. One of Carl's favourite times with Jan is when the baby has her morning sleep and Jan suggests that she and Carl play some games together. Jan has a big cotton bag which is tied at the top so that Carl cannot see inside. Jan regularly selects a collection of different objects inside the bag and the game begins when Carl feels deep inside and tries to guess what it is that he is feeling. Usually Jan has made a collection of things that feel very different, an apple perhaps, and a crayon, a prickly pine cone and a familiar toy car. Sometimes the game is different and instead of deciding what the objects are, Carl has to say what the objects feel like. Jan will ask, 'Find me something rough (or prickly or smooth or soft)' and Carl thinks that is really hard – but good fun too!

Another game that Jan has thought of is to put small amounts of different tasting things in small cups and ask Carl to close his eyes and guess what each taste is. Some are easy and enjoyable, like the grapes which are Carl's favourite and the tomato sauce that goes on his pasta but some, like the tiny grains of salt and the lemon juice he tried were not nearly so nice!

Carl also likes the outdoors games that they play when they take the baby out in the pushchair and go to the swings in the afternoons. Jan will talk to Carl along the way, saying perhaps 'Can you see a red car?' When they reach the park where the swings are Jan will sometimes say to Carl 'Can you find a very big leaf?' or 'If you stand very still you can hear that bird singing.' When they get home again, Jan and Carl often talk about all the things they have seen and heard during their walks, and then, when it is time for Carl's mum to come, Carl tells her all about his day.

This example of good, everyday practice heightens children's awareness of the sights, sounds, tastes and smells that are all around them but that they may not notice unless a trusted companion brings them to their attention. (See 'zone of proximal development', p. 9.)

Children's first response to their world is through their senses and so it is vital that children are helped to look carefully, listen attentively and experience a wide range of textures, smells and tastes. For children to be creative, they need to be familiar with a range of sensory experiences to be able to use what they have seen, heard, felt and smelled in their creative play. For example, when Carl next bakes buns with Jan and she asks him if he would like to make currant buns or cherry buns, he needs to know the difference between the taste of currants and cherries to make an informed choice and to begin to be creative in his cooking.

Learning story

- **Emotional learning.** Jan has made some basic learning into a game that Carl looks forward to. She has not only presented some useful learning in an active way that is a manageable challenge for Carl but also plays the game at a special time that the two of them share together when the baby is having her sleep. In this way, Carl feels that these are times just for him when his needs alone can be considered and that he is Jan's priority. Because the relationship between Jan and Carl is positive, warm and relaxed, he is eager to play the games that Jan suggests and his learning happens almost incidentally. (See 'key person', p. 25.)

- **Social learning.** Carl has learned that he can be valued, loved and have an enjoyable time when he is in Jan's family. Sometimes Jan's husband and children are at home when Carl is there, and the baby that Jan also cares for is another member of Jan's extended family. Through these positive experiences, Carl knows that being away from home and with different people can offer new and exciting things to learn about. He knows that families operate in different ways: they may eat differently, dress differently and behave to each other in different ways. The understanding that he has gained about different people gives him added confidence when he goes to play in his friends' homes and may well help him when he starts school as he has encountered groups of people outside his home with whom he feels comfortable.

- **Cognitive learning.** Jan has been skilful in teaching Carl about his senses in ways that are meaningful to him. She has not only ensured that he has learned about different textures but has also given him the words he needs to describe what he has felt, tasted or seen. For example, Jan calls the scratchy scourer 'rough'. Later on, she may ask him to pair two rough textures together and then find two shiny surfaces in another game that will give Carl an ever-widening range of experiences to draw on when he wishes to make his own creations. (See 'spiral curriculum', p. 14.) She may suggest to Carl that he tastes food from other cultures and perhaps play dressing up in clothes with which he is unfamiliar. All the while, Jan is introducing him to new situations that will widen his choices and give him a richer view of his world.

Look, listen and note

- Observe how much experience Carl has had with different scents, textures and sounds.

- Note whether he can identify those he has encountered and what level of support may be needed to help his development in this area.

- Check for any allergies or intolerances to any materials that might be presented to children for investigation.

Effective practice

- Make available a range of interesting new and familiar sensory experiences for children to explore.

- Ensure safety checks have been effectively carried out on anything a child may encounter and make quiet places available so that children engage for a long while and in a calm environment to gain the most from their investigations.

Planning

Plan to draw children's attention to everyday sights, smells, sounds and textures so that they become observant and get into the habit of noticing things. This could be a change in the weather, a flower in bud and one that is wilting or how ice melts in warm water. (See 'skills and attitudes of creativity', p. 21.)

Resourcing

- During walks outside collect natural materials such as wood, shells and stones.

- Shakers with different contents make different sounds.

- Previously collected materials of all sorts (particularly natural materials) can be used for colour matching.

The EYFS principles

The EYFS Principles are clear here too as Jan's recognition of Carl as a unique child is evidenced in her deep knowledge of him. She knows, for example, that he comes from a large and busy family and that it is sometimes hard for him to find those times when he has an adult's exclusive attention. She makes sure that she organises regular times when he and she spend some time together, and she has noticed how well he concentrates at these times and how much he looks forward to them. She is clearly pleased to see him and, by her manner towards him shows the attributes of one of his 'key people'. She is positive, warm, sensitive and responsive, and his trust in her is evidenced in his enthusiasm to join in the games and activities she suggests. She sometimes asks him to make up a game, thus helping him to feel that he can be 'in charge'. This positive relationship is genuine and mutual.

Jan has carefully thought through what she will do with Carl when he spends a day with her. Her time is dedicated to the needs of the children she is caring for and although time needs to be spent on everyday tasks such as washing up, shopping and tidying the toys, Carl joins in with these and learns very important lessons about keeping the environment clean and well organised. This is a setting where there is a good balance between times that are special for a young child and those regular tasks that need to be done. Each type of these activities presents rich learning opportunities that Jan exploits to the full. (See 'key person', p. 25.)

From 30–50 months

Development matters

- Use language and other forms of communication to share the things they create or to indicate personal satisfaction or frustration.

Key words
autonomy, collaboration, recall

Activity

Amir and Humzah are playing in the large dry sand in the outside area of the day-care setting they attend. Last week, one of the practitioners had hidden some 'treasure' in the sand, and the boys had spent most of a session finding it and then finding new places to hide it. Today there is no treasure hidden in the sand but Ali and Humzah are still intrigued by this 'hide and seek' game. They go to the creative area where they find some cardboard discs and some silver foil and set about making their own treasure. This turns out to be more difficult than they had imagined. The cardboard discs are too big and need cutting down to size, which is too hard for them to manage on their own. Anne, Humzah's key person, spots the trouble they are having and asks, 'Can I help you with that? What shape do you need?'

'Round ones', says Amir.

'Ah', says Anne, 'is it to make treasure?' Amir nods.

'Is this the right size?' asks Anne, cutting the circles smaller. 'How many do you need?'

'Lots', says Humzah.

'Well', says Anne, 'that will take me a very long time! Shall I make six and you can see if that's enough?'

The two boys collect and count the cardboard discs as they are finished and cover them with some silver foil.

'That looks like treasure now', says Amir, and he rushes outside to the sand to hide all the discs.

'I want some', says Humzah, following close behind.

'I'll hide them, and then you find them', suggests Amir. A rather heated debate follows but eventually the boys manage to share out the discs and take turns to hide them and find them. (See 'scaffolding', p. 16.)

Later, at a small group time, Anne asks the boys to tell the group what they have been doing all morning. Amir, who is the more vocal of the two friends, talks to the group about covering the discs with silver foil and hiding them in the dry sand for Humzah to find. Anne asks them questions such as 'Which bit was the most fun, hiding the treasure or finding it?', 'Which bits were the most difficult?' and 'Did you have enough treasure?'

Anne then says to Humzah, 'Would you like to play this game again tomorrow?', and, when Humzah nods, continues, 'Well, we must find somewhere safe to keep your treasure then, till you need it again.'

Anne then reads the group a story called *Dogger* about something that gets lost for a long while and is then found again and the group talks together about their experiences of losing and then finding something that is precious to them.

Learning story

- **Emotional learning.** The two boys show emotional self-confidence and independence by going to the creative area and finding the materials and tools they need to make their 'treasure' and also in accepting the help that they know they need. Anne helps them retain their ownership of the creative process by asking them what they specifically need help with and then allowing them to continue making the treasure independently. She respects their desire to play their game another day by suggesting that the 'treasure' is put in a safe place. In this way, the boys feel that they and their ideas are valued and that they have some autonomy about when they can play their game again. Anne follows up the game by sensitive use of a story about 'lost and found' so that all the children in the group can empathise with the feelings of delight in finding something important that has been out of sight for a while.

- **Social learning.** The two friends enjoy each other's company and play together most days. They have been learning about genuine collaboration in the 'hide and seek' game, which is a great strength in creative play. Anne knows both children well and understands that Humzah sometimes struggles to get his views heard when he plays with Amir as his language skills are not so advanced and his personality is not quite so ebullient. Anne supports him in his partnership with Amir by asking him his views and ideas thereby helping him to take an equal part in the game.

- **Cognitive learning.** There is a wealth of learning going on in this scene. Anne makes careful note of the conversation in the creative area as the discussion ranges around shapes and numbers. She remembers which child can count to six and who can divide the six discs equally between them. Later, at group time, Anne uses careful questioning to help the boys describe their game, modelling words that they might find helpful such as 'searching' and 'discovering' and encourages them to think critically about the process of creating the discs by asking them which part of the process was the most difficult. By asking the kinds of questions that Amir and Humzah are able to answer, they are helped to think more deeply about their activity, tell others what they have been doing and embed the concepts they have learned more securely in their minds. (See 'skills and attitudes of creativity', p. 21.)

Look, listen and note

- Observe that the two boys are learnning at a particularly high level when they are engaged in physical outdoor play.

- Note also that they play well together in an ever-maturing collaborative way.

Effective practice

- Respect and value children's own ideas and ensure a balance between enabling those and practitioners' planned activities.

- Recognise that children need ownership of their ideas for true creativity to flourish and make the materials available for them to follow their own play plans. (See 'play is intrinsically motivated', p. 16.)

Planning

Planning needs to respect children's ownership of their play so there is a need to recognise that equipment may be used flexibly and for a range of purposes and in different areas of the setting.

The EYFS principles

Anne's recognition of Amir and Humzah's friendship is an example of the EYFS principle of 'The Unique Child'. She not only values the strength of their friendship but understands how it needs to be supported to enable both children to progress. She respects their independence by choosing carefully when to intervene to move their play forward and when to stand back and observe and note what they have learned.

The environment is an enabling one, not only because the sand is being used to support children's imaginative and creative play but also in that it is the *children's* interests that are being followed rather than *adults'* ideas imposed on them. The setting's planning is flexible enough to allow the play to continue for as many days as the children's interest lasts. The respect and value that is given by staff to children's preferences is evidence of the positive and strong relationships that exist between adults and children in this setting.

From 40–60 months

Development matters

- Make comparisons and create new connections.

Key words

comparisons, celebrating diversity

Activity

At the nursery that Sally attends there is great excitement for today is carnival day! There is a visitor wearing a brightly coloured dress and a beautiful matching headdress. She is called Mary, and she has just taken some banana bread out of the nursery oven that she has cut into tiny pieces and offered to the children. Sally tries some and can taste the familiar banana flavour even though she has not eaten it in bread before. She tries another piece that Mary has left on a plate for children to help themselves. Next, Mary goes to the creative area, and Sally follows to see what she will do there. Mary takes some long strips of paper from her bag and begins to colour them with crayons. When several of them are coloured, she joins them together with the stapler and attaches them to a strong piece of cardboard which makes a handle.

'There', she says, 'this is my streamer to dance with.' She waves the streamer around her head to show the children how it moves in the air. Sally thinks it looks beautiful, and when Mary asks if any of the children would like to make one, Sally goes closer to Mary and says, 'Me. I would.' Soon, a group of children have made streamers, and Mary says, 'We are nearly ready for our carnival, but first we need some headdresses.' Out of her bag come some pieces of material like the one she herself is wearing, and Sally is one of the first children to volunteer to have one wrapped around her head so that she looks just like Mary. Not all the children want to dance, but Mary has also brought some musical instruments for them to play when it is time to dance in the carnival. There are drums to beat, finger harps, bamboo pipes to blow and big seed pods with the seeds still inside that rattle when shaken. Some of the instruments are delicate, and Mary checks that they are still working and that the seeds are secure inside the shaker before showing the children how to use them. One of the setting's practitioners stays with the instruments, helping the children to use them safely whilst Mary puts her music into the CD player. Sally listens to the African songs and watches Mary as she starts to dance, waving her streamer high above her head. The music is rhythmic and joyful, and soon Sally finds herself dancing behind Mary and waving her streamer as some of the other children bang and shake the instruments in time to the rhythm of the songs. Mary opens the setting door, and the carnival makes its way around the outside area before snaking back indoors and then outside once more. Sally is part of an excited trail of dancers and wants to go on dancing for ever.

However, Mary turns around and holds up her hands. 'Time to stop for a rest', she says, 'Carnival is hard work!'

The children make their way to their small groups, and Mary talks to each group in turn about the festivals and ceremonies that are a part of her cultural heritage.

Learning story

- **Emotional learning.** The nursery children have been helped to feel excited by and closer to Afro-Caribbean culture. Those children in the setting whose culture this is will have felt that they belong more securely to a setting where their festivals and ceremonies are celebrated in this way and will feel proud that their music and dance has been enjoyed by the whole nursery. (See 'adult's role', p. 21.)

- **Social learning.** Children in the setting have been helped to understand the social aspects of a different culture. As a nursery group, they have enjoyed making music, singing and dancing together in a day that was quite different from their usual nursery session. This joint venture, the creation of a carnival, required a range of different talents, interests and abilities to be combined and all the children could be involved in ways that suited them individually.

- **Cognitive learning.** There has been a significant amount of learning about a different way of living through this activity. Through the use of stories such as *Handa's Surprise,* pictures and artefacts, children will be enabled, in the days to come, to compare their lives with those of other children. Connections about lifestyles can be made, perhaps by discussions about carnivals the children have seen on television, and they may represent their own carnival experiences in drawings and paintings. A day such as this one gives the staff a rich resource to use when helping children to understand more deeply and to celebrate the differences that are a vital part of our multicultural heritage. (See 'making connections', p. 6.)

Look, listen and note

Practitioners will have noted the need to raise children's awareness of cultural diversity, and a day such as this will be only a part of planning to ensure their continuing understanding and valuing of the richness of cultural differences.

Effective practice

Follow-up activities such as stories, poems, paintings and posters will be needed to help children appreciate how lives are lived in different ways.

Planning

Plan any event on two levels:

1   A one-off event such as a visit from someone who can raise awareness of a new or different skill or culture helps children to make connections to the new ideas on their own.

2   Ensure that your planning covers follow-up activities after the main event has finished.

Resourcing

Useful additions would be cooking materials, dressing-up clothes together with artefacts, stories and pictures of any culture being explored both on display and being used.

📖   Browne, E. (1995) *Handa's Surprise,* London: Walker.

⬡⬡⬡ The EYFS principles

In recognising the principles of the EYFS the celebration of a different culture gives value to those children whose culture this is. Their unique ways of living are respected, and the setting in general is a richer place because of this positive attitude to diversity. The fact that this celebration had been planned into the curriculum indicates an environment that enables children from a range of cultures to feel accepted and equal members of the setting. The staff's positive professional relationships with each other and with the children have helped this to be a day that everyone enjoyed. It should be noted here, perhaps, that if the setting has children of only one culture, it is even more vital for recognition of a range of cultures and faiths to be put in place so that these children are better prepared to take their place in our multicultural world.

Exploring media and materials

From birth–11 months

Activity

Food is something that young babies come into contact with every day! Eating becomes a continuous element of their lives, and different foods evoke very different responses. As such, food can be thought of as a medium that can be used creatively.

Lauren is eleven months old and is at a day-care setting three days a week. The practitioners have talked with her family about her feeding needs and her preferences and are following the routine that Lauren is used to very closely. She very much enjoys her mid-morning bottle of milk which soothes and comforts her and settles her for her day-time sleep. At lunchtime she is beginning to reject spoon-feeding by turning her head away and showing that she wants to feed herself. The setting's staff allow her to use either her fingers or a spoon to pick up her food, although this makes feeding time a long process and usually makes a lot of mess! It is worth the effort as not only will Lauren eat much more if allowed to feed herself, she clearly enjoys playing with the different textures of the food that she is given. Today, Jennie gives Lauren a new taste to try after her pasta, a tiny piece of broccoli. Jennie stays with Lauren to encourage her to try it and smiles at her as Lauren looks carefully at it, lifts it to her face to feel, smell and taste. It looks interesting to Lauren, and she puts it in her mouth where it stays for a while. Then, her face screws up and the broccoli comes out again, ending up in the tray of her bib.

'Oh dear', says Jennie, 'not so good? Another day, perhaps', and gives Lauren her fruit. Lauren pushes her fruit this way and that and enjoys watching it travel across the table before eating it all up.

Jennie says, 'Yum, yum, that fruit is my favourite', and then gives her a small pot of yoghurt and a spoon. Lauren uses the spoon for a while to eat her yoghurt but then dips her finger into the yogurt and watches the yoghurt drop off her finger on to the table. She draws her finger to and fro through the yogurt, making marks in it and watching intently as she does so. Jennie allows this to continue and occasionally intervenes by giving Lauren a spoonful of yogurt so that she is sure that the majority is eaten. This way, Jennie ensures that there is a balance between Lauren eating a good meal and also registering her independence and her preferences.

Feeding very small children can be an emotional battleground! However, it is a wise carer who can use this daily routine to help children explore new textures and tastes and to develop their preferences and yet curb the understandable desire to see each meal calmly and completely eaten.

Learning story

- **Emotional learning.** For the adult who has lovingly cooked a new food to widen their baby's range of foods, it can be heartbreaking to see it rejected. The baby, however, is just registering a reaction to something unfamiliar, and Jennie responds lightly by accepting Lauren's rejection but asserting that the new taste will be offered again. Very often, on the second or third attempt, the taste is not so unfamiliar and the baby will accept the new food.

  Jennie also shows wisdom in tolerating Lauren's wish to make marks in her yogurt. She recognises that Lauren is learning a new sensation and that it is through these routine events that young babies can begin to explore early creativity and that Lauren's informed choices about what textures and tastes she prefers are based on experiences such as these. (See 'spiral curriculum', p. 14.)

- **Social learning.** The companionship that Jennie offers as Lauren's key person gives Lauren the confidence to try out new experiences as well as the freedom to express her own opinions without fear of rejection. The fact that other babies with whom Lauren is familiar are also trying out new things, by discovering different textures and materials through their daily routines and through their play, contributes to an expectation that this is a place where opportunities for creativity are welcomed and valued.

- **Cognitive learning.** Lauren is clearly learning about the sight, feel, taste and texture of new foods and is developing the preferences that we all have for some of them. She is also learning that eating is a pleasurable and a sociable activity where groups of trusted friends gather together to chat over the day's events while eating (a routine which a wise family will continue through until the end of the teenage years!). The attractive presentation of the food that Lauren is offered at this stage in her life may well help to create a positive view of food that may inspire her later on to be a creative cook.

Look, listen and note

- Note how each baby responds to new food.

- Watch as each child explores the texture and taste of familiar and new foods and note what is eaten and which are preferred.

- Take note of any dietary restrictions, both medical and cultural, for each child.

Effective practice

- The majority of food that is given to babies should be well known and liked with only tiny amounts of a new taste added.

- A lot of time needs to be given for them to explore new food with all their senses.

- Encouragement is also needed at any attempt to try something unfamiliar, and babies who reject a new taste shouldn't be chided. Just offer it again another day.

- Allow babies to play with food and to feed themselves.

Planning

Part of ongoing individual planning should ensure that each baby has the food that they enjoy for a majority of the time. Plan to have some small finger food to encourage independent feeding.

Resourcing

- A range of food with different textures such as yoghurt, fruit and pasta.

- A range of sweet and savoury foods with all food having a well balanced nutritional content.

- Plenty of time.

- Plenty of bibs or 'cover ups' so spillage can be seen as an acceptable part of experimentation and expressing preferences.

- Small amounts of food as a try-out with more available if successful.

⬡ The EYFS principles

The EYFS themes can be seen in this example as Jennie respects Lauren's individuality as she expresses her choices and preferences for certain types of food. Whilst following these choices Jennie tries to move Lauren's learning on by offering, in a sensitive way, new tastes and textures. The positive ethos in the setting is demonstrated by the amount of time that the adults are prepared to give to mealtimes and the tolerance they show for children's dabbling and experimenting with their food. The environment supports this ethos by following each child's home routines as much as practically possible and by catering for a full range of dietary requirements.

From 8–20 months

Development matters

● Explore and experiment with a range of media using the whole body.

Key words

experiencing, senses

Activity

Hassam is eighteen months old and attends his nursery every afternoon. On this particular day, Sam, the practitioner, has made some play dough. Whilst it was cooking Sam has added a few drops of lavender oil so that when it reaches the table it smells of lavender as well as being warm to the touch. Hassam rubs his hands gently over his piece of dough, enjoying the warmth.

Sam says, 'How does it feel, Hassam?'

Hassam says, 'Hot.'

Sam replies, 'That's right, its lovely and warm isn't it? Can you smell it too? Mmmm, that smells good.'

Hassam spends several minutes, alongside other toddlers at the dough table, prodding and smelling the warm play dough. He puts a piece up to his cheek to feel it in a different way and then begins squeezing it hard between his fingers. There are no implements to roll the dough as practitioners want the very young children to experience the dough with their hands and fingers first before giving them tools to use. (See 'spiral curriculum', p. 14.)

After ten minutes or so, Sam brings some shells and puts them on the table beside the dough.

'Look Hassam', he says. 'Look what happens if I press the shell into the dough. Can you see the shape the shell has made in the dough? Would you like to try that?'

Hassam picks up a shell and tries to make an imprint on the dough but without success.

'You have to press really hard, Hassam, like this', explains Sam and shows Hassam once again how to press the shell into the dough. Hassam tries again with a little more success this time, but Sam says, 'I think that's really hard' and goes to fetch some small sticks that will make impressions in the dough as well.

Experiencing properties of materials

Hassam finds this much easier and spends a long time poking his sticks into the dough, pulling them out and looking at the dough that remains stuck on his sticks.

Learning story

- **Emotional learning.** This activity is both soothing and safe. There is no end product expected and no complex implement for the toddlers to have to manipulate. At a later date, Sam will introduce more challenging ways of playing with the dough but as it is a nearly new experience to Hassam, he needs to experience its properties with his senses.

  Sam decided that he needed to present it as a manageable challenge. Hassam clearly enjoyed smelling, touching and squeezing the dough and the satisfaction of succeeding to make impressions in it with the small sticks. Having the company of Sam, whom he trusts, also gives him the confidence to try something that Sam suggests and to cope with failure if the experiment is not too successful.

- **Social learning.** Hassam is enjoying this activity in the company of children he sees every day and a practitioner who he knows well and trusts. Children are often more courageous at trying new things if they can see others trying them too and are in familiar situations where they know that there will not be unreasonable expectations made of them.

- **Cognitive learning.** This is a rich learning experience for Hassam. He has played with dough once or twice before but not with warm dough or dough that is scented. At his setting, his range of experiences is being extended as the staff vary the temperature, colour and texture of the play dough. This is not an activity where practitioners expect something to be made; it is purely about experiencing possibilities and the properties of the materials on offer.

It is important, especially with very young children, for practitioners to be very clear about what their learning intentions are when presenting media for exploration. If learning expectations are muddled, practitioners may be confused about an activity's expectations and be tempted to always expect an end product when, in fact, the exploring stage of the materials is a vital first step. That is not to say that children with more experience should be denied the opportunity to take their learning further but that there should be appropriate value given to the early stages of exploring media and materials that are new and different. (See 'key aspects of play' 1, p. 15.)

Look, listen and note

Take note of the level at which children are understanding and benefiting from the activity as individuals and adjust it accordingly.

Effective practice

Keep supplies of resources easily available to ensure children remain interested and successful.

Planning

Planning is based on the observation staff have made of children's levels of development and so know how to offer materials at the correct level so as to encourage building interest.

Resourcing

Make different kinds of dough, baked and unbaked. For variety, add salt, colour and seeds and lavender oil for smell. There are numerous recipes for dough on the Internet.

⬡ The EYFS principles

Sam realised that Hassam is at a unique point in his stage of learning about the dough. There are other toddlers in the setting who are at a similar stage to Hassam in their enjoyment of exploring the properties of play dough but who are not ready to make something representational with it. Sam has presented the play dough in a way that exactly meets these children's learning needs, and he will find that because of this careful matching, the children may well be engaged intently in the activity for a long while. This ability that Sam has to match an activity to the interests and level of development of a child is a skill which has a huge impact on the way in which Hassam and his friends will approach new learning. (See 'zone of proximal development', p. 9.) ©

The care and affection that Sam shows towards Hassam is evident in his adjustment of the activity when the shells are seen to be too challenging and the small sticks are used instead as successful alternative. Note also that there is no blame attached to Hassam for the apparent failure; Sam acknowledges straight away that this new task is not well matched to Sam's stage of development by saying 'That's really hard.' This is a sign of his sensitivity and responsiveness. The environment is seen to be enabling as shells, sticks and other interesting natural materials are easily accessible for Sam to use with his group of toddlers.

From 16–26 months

Development matters

- Create and experiment with blocks, colours and marks.

Key words

mark-making, schemas

Activity

Kieran, at just over two, has shown a consistent resistance to mark-making. His parents, both interior designers, have watched his artistic development with interest and regularly give him crayons and paint brushes in the hopes that he will begin to show an interest and, perhaps, an early talent as they did. They ask his nursery staff to keep any evidence of his mark-making ability but, as yet, there is nothing to see, as he prefers to spend his time outside with the wheeled toys or playing on the big apparatus, climbing, jumping and balancing. He is skilled at these activities and is beginning to show signs of a preference for being either 'up high' or 'down low' as he crawls and climbs with ever more confidence. Staff think that Kieran is showing evidence of schematic play and that he is enjoying learning about how it feels to be high up at the top of the climbing equipment and the contrast of being low down as he crawls through the tunnel. (See 'schemas', p. 16.)

Often, the nursery staff put chalks, big brushes and small buckets of water in the garden. One day, Kieran moves towards these and watches other children making marks with the chalks on the ground and then washing them off with the wet brushes. After watching for a long while, Kieran picks up a chalk and draws a long, straight line on the ground. He washes it off straight away, laughs and jumps up and down with delight. Soon he is drawing another and then another until there are rows of straight lines drawn in a range of colours. As a member of the nursery staff comes towards him to encourage his new skill of mark-making, he quickly washes the lines off and moves back to the crawling tunnel.

Learning story

- **Emotional learning.** It is possible to suggest that Kieran may, indeed, have considerable artistic talent as his parents hope, but that he is feeling under some pressure to produce evidence of it before he is ready.

  Settings that provide ways for children to make marks which are temporary help children to feel less pressured as the children are in control over their marks and can wash them away before others can judge them to be 'right' or 'wrong' (as we saw with Jo, p. 5). At a later stage, children's first letters are often made in this informal way, thus building their confidence until they feel ready to show others, and in particular adults, their creative efforts. Children learn very early that adults attach great importance to marks on paper and sometimes feel intimidated by the pressure to produce a picture or some 'writing'.

- **Social learning.** It is particularly helpful to Kieran that the setting he attends recognises the value of 'incidental' mark-making and provides the activity of the paint brushes and water on a regular basis. The fact that it is valued as an activity and that Kieran can drop in and out of it as he wishes gives him exactly the opportunity he needs; to practise little and often until he feels confident enough to show the end results to someone else. Indeed, it may be that the first person he shows his drawings to will be a friend, rather than an adult. In the larger environment of the early years setting, children often see new and different learning opportunities that they can try out without feeling under any pressure and can seek and receive a range of opinions on their efforts. (See 'key aspects of play', p. 15.)

- **Cognitive learning.** This activity is helping Kieran to understand that marks do not have to be made only on paper. More informal marks can be made with crayons, chalks, paint and even water. He will learn that marks made with water outside will dry out on sunny days and that creative marks can be made on other surfaces such as the ground or a chalk board. Marks can be made into an individual creation by just one child or they can made as a contribution to a project which several children add to, making a collaborative venture. He will discover that creativity is a fluid process and ideas will come and go. A picture or pattern, for example, will most probably change during the process of its creation and be different at the end from how the child may have thought of it at the start. It is unwise, therefore, to try to make young children talk about their intentions as this can constrain their imagination.

Look, listen and note

- Watch carefully to see what creative interests each particular child has, whether it is artistic, musical or imaginative play.

- Note whether they are confident or whether they seem constrained by any anxieties and think through ways to support their creative development at whatever level they are at.

Effective practice

- Ensure that resources are fit for purpose, can be used for a range of purposes and that children can access them easily.

- Liaise with parents about the value of informal mark-making and the dangers of making writing and drawing too formal too soon.

Planning

When planning for children's mark-making, include less orthodox ways of making marks, recognising that these are just as valid as pencil marks on paper.

Resourcing

- Dry sand for marks made with fingers.

- Paint and large sheets of paper or old cardboard boxes for use with big brushes.

- Water in small buckets for making marks on playgrounds.

- Opportunities for children to make patterns using paint, pencils and crayons.

The EYFS principles

The EYFS Principles are particularly helpful in supporting children in their creative development. The emphasis that the theme 'A Unique Child' places on recognising children's ability to be capable, confident and self-assured assists practitioners to respect children's creations and to resist any temptation to impose on children their own ideas. One of the keys to creativity is that children have to be in control of what they are creating. Adults must be sensitive to this and never expect a child to create to an adult's agenda; the child's creation must be respected and valued in its own right. When it is finished, it has to be finished to the child's satisfaction and not to the satisfaction of the adult. The practitioner who knows each child best, the key person, will be best placed to offer any support and to encourage and, perhaps most importantly, will know when to simply observe and note the child's creative actions. The environment that enables children's creativity to flourish is the one that provides a wide range of materials in good condition with which children can create, in ways that *they* choose and adults who appreciate this as the golden rule of early creativity, which is that the *process of creating* is more important than the production of an end result. Remember that this is stated quite clearly in the principles as 'It is difficult for children to make creative connections in learning when colouring in a worksheet or making a Diwali card just like everyone else's' (DfES 2007: card 4.3). (See Activities and provision, p. 17.)

From 22–36 months

Development matters

- Begin to combine movement, materials, media or marks.

Key words

senses, raising awareness

Activity

One summer morning, staff in an inner-city setting have added some flowers to the warm water trough. One adult stays with the water play as the children approach it. Several children come close but are cautious of the unfamiliar contents of the trough and hang back, waiting to see what might happen. Their curiosity is aroused, but they are unsure what response to make to what they can see in the trough.

Susie, the adult, says, 'We've put some flowers in the water today; don't they look different when they float around in the water?' She dabbles her hand in the warm water and the children watch as the flowers begin to move gently around on the surface.

'Would you like to try that?' she asks, and soon two of the children are touching the flowers, and Susie talks to them about how different they look in water. She shows them some dry flowers that she has brought into the setting, and the children look at and feel the difference between wet and dry petals. Susie shows the children some herbs that she has brought, and they smell them as she gives each its name. She suggests that the herbs, too, could be put in the water trough, which the children do with more enthusiasm as they are now intrigued by this new activity. Susie and the children discuss the smells that the herbs make and whether the smells are stronger in water. One child knows that his mummy uses one of the herbs for cooking, and Susie suggests that next time they make 'nursery soup' they could add some of the herbs in too. One child, Janie, asks if she can collect some more flowers to drop into the water from the outdoor area, and Susie liaises with the staff who are outside to help Janie and also to limit her enthusiasm for picking flowers! Soon the trough has flowers, herbs, grasses and leaves floating on the water with the children eagerly discussing how they look, feel and smell.

This activity is repeated for a few days with an ever-wider number of children taking part. The setting staff put books with pictures of flowers and herbs on display and talk to the children at group time about how artists have drawn and painted flowers, herbs and leaves. The children are shown good-quality reproductions of well-known paintings, and lively discussions take place about which ones are liked best.

One child brings from home his mother's flower press and shows the group some carefully pressed leaves and flowers.

The aim of this activity is to raise children's awareness of things that may inspire them, perhaps at a later date, to represent what interests and intrigues them.

Learning story

- **Emotional learning.** Children respond well to being introduced to a range of natural materials as one of young children's earliest responses to the world is through their senses. It is satisfying to be able to appreciate beauty through touch, sight and scent, and they can be encouraged to explore how they feel about a range of natural objects. To be creative enough to use a wide range of materials in paintings, drawings or collage, children need to be very familiar with the objects to be represented and very confident in a range of techniques that can be used. (See 'spiral curriculum', p. 14.)

- **Social learning.** Becoming familiar with beautiful and interesting objects is a first step to creativity. The sensitivity that the setting staff show in collecting and presenting these materials in ways that will inspire children increases children's awareness of the possibilities to represent these objects. The close and supportive relationship that the staff have with each other and with the children ensures that such opportunities are maximised. The wide range of families that attend the setting allows for objects to be contributed from families whose interest may have been aroused by their children's learning.

- **Cognitive learning.** Before children can be expected to use natural materials as an inspiration for drawings, paintings or collage, much time has to be spent in activities such as this one; playing with the objects, exploring their properties and comparing, for example, one flower with another or one leaf with another. Remember Jo, in Chapter 1, who had spent many sessions playing with scissors, glue and Sellotape before he was ready to create his car. (See p. 5.)

Central to creativity is the skill of observation, without which representation, in particular, is impossible. So, although at the end of this activity there is no end product, no picture to put on the setting's wall or in a child's folder, a secure basis has been laid for their future creative development. Children at this stage have very few inhibitions and, if shown great works of art, such as Van Gogh's *Sunflowers* or Monet's *Water Lilies,* will not show the usual adult response of 'I couldn't possibly do that.' With the background of experiences such as that described here and effective support and resourcing, children may well feel confident enough to 'have a go' in the same way that they do with writing, singing, climbing and all their other activities. It is this positive attitude, or disposition, that is important to encourage here rather than the necessity to represent with accuracy. (See 'mastery learner', p. 9.)

Look, listen and note

This activity may need a change of adult input as it becomes more familiar to the children. At first, an adult will probably be needed to guide the play and to suggest things about the flowers to think and talk about. As the children become more accustomed to the activity, the adult may want to observe the play, noting which children appear to need support in their creative development and which are more confident. Note also how the activity may be extended to cater for children's individual interests and needs and be aware of possible hazards such as inedible objects being tasted or unsuitable objects being added to the water.

Effective practice

- This primarily consists of widening children's experiences with natural objects that they may not have previously encountered.

- Effective practitioners are always on the lookout for objects that may arouse children's curiosity and cause them to think more deeply.

- Effective practice also involves understanding that play and exploration are key forerunners of drawing and painting and that the process of creating is more important than the end product.

Planning

Plan to interest children by introducing unusual combinations of objects – in this case flowers or herbs and water. Collage work, for example, can combine materials attached to a piece of paper with decoration.

The EYFS principles

The concept of creativity is unique to each child, and each child responds differently to the stimuli that setting staff present. There will be family and cultural differences to influence how children feel about particular objects that they are given to look at and play with. This range gives setting staff a rich diversity to draw on as children's preferences and interests are discussed and compared. Children also vary in their abilities to observe, to compare and to use resources. Staff need to support children individually according to their individual needs and to be wary of expecting drawings and paintings as a result of these early experiences. (See 'key person', p. 25.)

The nature of the positive relationships within the setting is evidenced by the way that children deal with encountering a new experience. In the scenario, the staff knew that the children would be unsure of how to respond to the flowers in the water and so had planned to have Susie there to encourage them and to offer language to describe their experiences. As the children became more familiar with the flowers in the water trough, the adult support would perhaps be changed to one of observing and noting. The environment also responds to the children's needs and interests by the increase in the number of days that the activity was made available and by encouraging children to collect other natural objects such as grasses and leaves to drop into the trough. There are plenty of flowers and herbs for the children to look at and play with which avoids the frustration of running out of materials. The activity is therefore planned to be well resourced and flexible. (See 'rich environment', p. 7.)

From 30–50 months

Development matters

● Explore colour and begin to differentiate between colours.

Key words
cooperative play, small motor skills

Activity

Practitioners in Jade's setting had planned to introduce children to a range of colours and textures through weaving. During the previous weeks, they had collected a wide selection of ribbons, wool and string. Nick, one of the staff, brought a cane cone that he had been using to support the sweet peas he grew in his garden into the setting. He had realised the potential of the cone as something that young children could weave things through with a certain degree of success. He and other staff members began weaving some ribbons through the cone and were rather surprised at how satisfying they found the experience!

They also discovered that by working together and discussing the positioning of different shades of ribbons and wool they had created a rather attractive piece of weaving, and they decided to leave it to show the children when they arrived in the setting. At the start of the session, the now colourful cone was the centre of attention. Children viewed it from every angle, and Nick explained that he had brought it in from home and that he and the other staff had decorated it. Jade wanted to add a ribbon, and Nick found her a space that had been left empty. Carefully Jade pushed her green ribbon through the cane and out again and kept weaving her ribbon until it reached almost all the way around the cone. When she had finished, several other children wanted to try weaving too so Nick removed the staff's ribbons to leave the children plenty of space. He assured them that the cone would be staying at the setting for a long time so that everyone could try weaving, and he stayed with the activity for a while to give those who needed it help to thread the ribbons, wool and string through the holes in the cone.

The cone stayed in the setting for several weeks, with children adding to it whenever they wished. One day, a child found some long grass on the way to nursery and wove it through the cone. (See 'enough time', p. 10.)

This inspired some children to find other grasses and leaves in the outside area that they could use and so the cone took on a different appearance as it became woven with natural materials. Staff took some photos of the completed weaving as well as work in progress to use as part of their assessment procedure.

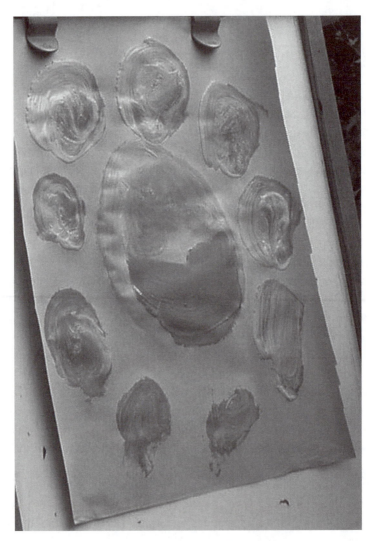

Differentiating colours and textures

Learning story

- **Emotional learning.** This learning activity has been carefully arranged to be non-threatening. Although a new experience for the children, there are no right or wrong ways to thread ribbons and so children can feel excited by the challenge it offers without fearing failure. As it is to be in the setting for an extended period of time, they can revisit the experience, gaining confidence and competence each time. (See 'right and wrong answers', p. 10.)

- **Social learning.** This activity also lends itself to cooperation, offering an opportunity for children to make a weaving that is the result of joint thinking and planning. This is a satisfying experience for those children who are ready to join in a cooperative creative venture with their friends.

- **Cognitive learning.** Children are invited to learn about differentiating between colour, textures and the properties of materials that make them suitable for weaving. For example, grasses and leaves need to be long and thin in shape to weave successfully, and children need to begin to make those judgements when choosing which materials to weave. It presents opportunities for children to discuss with staff which colours and textures might look attractive together and so encourage the beginnings of ideas about design. The weaving cone also helps to develop children's small manipulative skills within a genuinely creative activity.

Look, listen and note

- Staff roles will need to be flexible for this activity. They will need to observe which children need help in joining what may be a busy and popular pastime and to note which children are ready to take part in a joint creation with friends.

- To be successful, the weaving should be allowed to operate at many levels, from simple to complex, so that children at all stages of development can use it with a degree of satisfaction. (See 'spiral curriculum', p. 14.)

Effective practice

- Attractive and readily available resources are necessary for the weaving to be successful.

- Children should be able to access an ever-widening range of materials so that they can make increasingly informed choices about what they would like to use relating to their own ideas.

- Practitioners should encourage children to bring their own materials to weave, from the outside area or from home, and to extend children's knowledge of weaving by showing them other examples of weaving such as mats, tapestry or embroidery. They can also provide different articles to use as looms.

Planning

Plan to develop children's small motor skills at the same time as developing their creative skills.

Resourcing

- Allow children to create patterns in paper or card using a hole punch to create the holes and then to thread wool, ribbon, grasses, etc., through them.

- Keep a range of wools, strings and ribbons for children to use to weave.

- Older children, appropriately supervised, can weave through hessian using a blunt needle.

The EYFS principles

The EYFS themes are reflected here in that children are able to try the weaving activity at a level and in a way that suits their individual developmental needs, perhaps by watching what other children are doing or by organising a cooperative project with friends. Staff need to be flexible in their approach, as we saw from Nick's interaction. Staff will need to be available to support some children who are new to the process of threading but also be prepared to leave children to follow their own creative ideas as and when they emerge. The flexible environment will ensure that the cone is made available for children to use for some weeks so that they can revisit the activity and their expertise can develop over time.

From 40–60 months

Development matters

- Explore what happens when they mix colours.

- Choose particular colours to use for a purpose.

Key words
representation, cross-curricular

Activity

In the early spring at Kyle's reception class, teachers have planned to construct a large-scale interactive display to illustrate how plants grow from seeds. They have linked this activity with one of the children's favourite stories, *Jack and the Beanstalk*. Real beans have been planted, and, as they have grown, staff have discussed with children the shapes and shades of green of the leaves. As part of their planning process, it was decided to recreate the beanstalk high enough to reach the ceiling, using paints, paper and cardboard. Kyle had particularly enjoyed listening to the story and was one of the first children at the painting table when Nicola, the practitioner, began to talk to the children about how the huge beanstalk might be created.

On the painting table she had put yellow, blue, white and black powder paints, plastic dishes, a selection of brushes and some pieces of white paper, pencils and erasers. She brought one of the growing beans to the painting table so that children could carefully observe the colour and shape of the stalk and leaves. (See 'stages of creativity', p. 12.)

'Could anyone draw a picture of the beanstalk before we start making it so that we know what it might look like?' she asked. Several children took pencils and pieces of paper and began to draw their ideas of how the beanstalk might look. Nicola called these drawings 'plans' and pinned them to the wall near the painting table. She suggested that they begin with the stalk and she made a curved shape from the cardboard.

'What colour does the stalk need to be?' she asked.

'Green', chorused the eager group of painters, brushes ready to cover the stalk in green paint.

'Well', said Nicola, 'we need to mix our own colour green to make sure that it is just the colour we need.'

As the children had already had a lot of practice at paint-mixing, most knew that they needed to mix a lot of yellow with a tiny bit of blue to make green. What was new to most of them, however, was the idea of shading the green by adding a little black to make it darker or white to make it lighter. After much experimentation by mixing paint in the plastic dishes and much checking on the colour of the growing beans, they decided that they had mixed just the right colour for the stalk and it was duly painted! With the variety of greens that were left from their experiments, the children painted leaves for their beanstalk, each choosing either a lighter or darker shade of green for his or her leaf. As the project progressed over the coming days, the staff attached the stalk to the setting's walls, and each child's leaf was added until the beanstalk had 'grown' up to the ceiling and around the walls. Incidentally, this particular project developed in a rather unusual way. One child brought an enormous leaf he had found lying in the park in to the class. He was excited as it had a tiny spider still attached to the back of the leaf. Very soon, he had made a spider out of paper, coloured it and hidden it on the back of his painted leaf on the beanstalk and soon many children wanted to paint insects to attach to their beanstalk leaves. Although not part of the Jack and the Beanstalk story, this maintained their interest in and commitment to the project. (See 'spontaneous play', p. 17.)

Many children's imagination is fired by a project such as this. Although much close supervision by adults is required to achieve a creation of this kind, a sensitive sharing of ownership between the adults and the children ensures that the children feel that the beanstalk is 'theirs'. This is a necessity to maintain the children's commitment as they will quickly lose the desire to add to the beanstalk or to continue talking about the story if they feel that it is wholly the teacher's project. (See 'children's ownership', p. 15.)

Learning story

- **Emotional learning.** Children are able to join in this activity at a range of different levels, from watching the beanstalk change as new things are added to perhaps making up their own stories about who might live at the top! There are no right or wrong contributions, and children can feel confident to offer as much or as little as they wish. However, it is unlikely that any child will feel uninterested in a learning activity that is presented in this format; it is more likely that ideas will flow on a daily basis and that children will engage in a deep level of thinking. (See 'skills and attitudes of creativity', p. 21.)

- **Social learning.** The early years setting provides excellent opportunities for large-scale creations such as this. The range of interests and talents amongst both the children and the adults makes it possible for a genuine sharing of ideas to flourish which results in a high level of satisfaction and joint pride in their achievements.

- **Cognitive learning.** Much of the EYFS curriculum can be effectively taught through this project as it provides opportunities for children to learn about size and shape (problem-solving, reasoning and numeracy), develop their spoken language skills (communication, language and literacy), and to learn more about how plants grow (knowledge and understanding of the world). This style of teaching is sometimes known as 'cross-curricular' as there are many different types of learning embedded within it from all areas of the curriculum. Creatively, children are able to develop their own ideas from first-hand practical experiences as well as learn some of the skills associated with creativity, such as paint-mixing, designing, cutting and working on a large scale and cooperative collage. (See 'creativity in the wider curriculum', p. 20.)

Look, listen and note

As well as noting children's interest in this activity and the learning that is happening across the curriculum, staff will need to monitor the project itself carefully. Too much adult control will lessen children's interest and engagement; yet too little support and interaction will leave children unable to participate to their satisfaction as resources such as paint and glue need careful supervision.

Effective practice

- Appropriate practitioner support is key to success in a project such as this.

- Careful planning and timetabling will be needed to make sure that enough adult support is on hand and enough preparation time will enable resources to be sufficient in quantity and easily accessible before the cutting and painting begins.

- Work with the children beforehand will also be needed for them to engage with the creation. They need to have listened to stories about beans growing and if possible, to have grown their own.

- Such a project will not be successful with very young children unless they can link it to some previous first-hand experience. (See 'key aspects of play', p. 15.)

Planning

Careful whole-staff planning is necessary to ensure that the correct level of adult support is available. The roles of the adults need to be carefully considered to maintain children's enthusiasm but not to overpower children's intentions. Consider the timetabling implications of a large-scale project in terms of where and when the painting can take place without too much interruption.

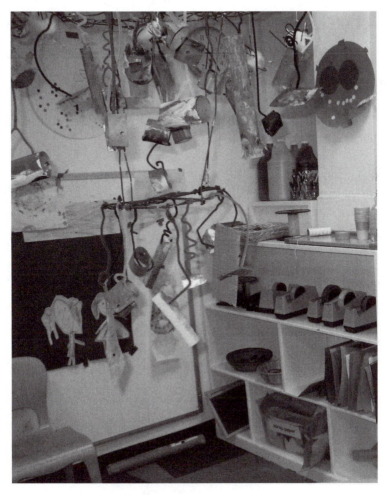

Everyday creative resources

Resourcing

Everyday creative resources such as powder paint, scissors, glue, stapler, cardboard, pencils, erasers and paper.

The EYFS principles

As each child contributes according to his or her own interests and level of development to the beanstalk, every child's uniqueness is respected and valued. Some children will, therefore, be at the level of watching and taking an interest in the project whereas others will be making significant contributions and taking responsibility for the 'growth' of the beanstalk in the class. (See 'spiral curriculum', p. 14.)

The relationships between the staff and the children are sensitive and responsive enough to recognise the children's range of talents and interests so that they can engage them appropriately and provide activities that will provide achievable challenges. The adults' roles will need to be flexible as staff move between close practical support in the production of the collage and noting and observing those children who may need support in developing the necessary skills to be able to partake. The environment will enable children to take an active part in the project if the necessary resources are ready in good time, they are attractive and within children's easy reach.

3 | Creating music and dance

From birth–11 months

> ### Development matters
>
> - Respond to a range of familiar sounds, for example, turning to a sound source such as a voice.
>
> - Explore colour and begin to differentiate between colours.
>
> ### Key words
> stimulating, enjoyable shared music-making

Activity

Robert, at eight months, is enjoying the wider world that is opening up to him now that he is sitting up securely and beginning to move around. As Suzanne, his key person at his nursery comes into view, he lifts up his arms and smiles at her. 'Are you coming up?' asks Suzanne, smiling back. She lifts him on to her lap facing her and asks, 'Shall we sing "Row, Row, Row, the Boat"?' Robert holds out his arms again; Suzanne holds them, and soon they are rowing down the imaginary river with Suzanne singing and rocking herself and Robert 'gently down the stream'. Robert's body language shows Suzanne how much he is enjoying this combination of movement and song and she asks 'Again?' There are several more trips down the stream before

Suzanne changes the mood a little and starts to sing 'This Is the Way the Ladies Ride', bouncing Robert more vigorously as the rhyme progresses until he falls 'down into the ditch' by being carefully slid on to the floor at the end. There is much laughter, and it is clear that both Suzanne and Robert are enjoying these action rhymes.

Learning story

- **Emotional learning.** Robert feels safe and secure when being rocked to and fro or bounced up and down as it is with Suzanne that these exciting actions take place. Very young babies will enjoy physical movement that they cannot achieve on their own if it is with a person they love and trust. He is learning that music and movement are a satisfying combination and that he feels valued by being an equal partner in the process of the actions. (See 'key person', p. 25.)

  He is beginning to learn that music is stimulating as well as comforting and, like stories, most satisfying when carried out with people who are important to him. Singing with babies enables them to experience a range of moods with their carer, from excitement (as in 'This Is the Way the Ladies Ride'), to a gentle calm (such as 'Row, Row, Row Your Boat').

- **Social learning.** Although music and dance can be solitary occupations, they are often part of a joint creative process. A significant part of the joy of music-making is the sharing of the experience with others and the sense of belonging and companionship that results from contributing to a paired or group creative experience.

- **Cognitive learning.** Robert is learning to listen, anticipate, discriminate and memorise. He is learning the order in which the actions happen and begins to understand the variation that Suzanne uses in pitch, dynamics and tempo. He will learn how music encourages the body to move rhythmically and how body movements and music fit satisfyingly together.

Look, listen and note

- A close knowledge of each young baby's particular interests will help practitioners to key in to an individual baby's learning needs and level of development (See 'zone of proximal development', p. 9.)

- Informal conversations with parents and carers will often give a wealth of information about songs sung at home and which are particular favourites.

- Practitioners should aim to extend babies' repertoires of rhymes and songs as these form the basis of many early picture and storybooks.

Effective practice

- The one skill an adult does *not* need when singing with babies is to be able to sing in tune! Other adults are not the audience here, and very young children cannot tell and do not mind whether each note is sung accurately. At this stage, music-making is most valuable as a shared, emotionally enjoyable, experience which helps children begin to interpret their world through the medium of music.

- Good collections of easily accessible nursery rhymes are essential, and, for practitioners who may feel they do not know enough rhymes, there are excellent CDs on the market to help widen their selection.

- Singing does not have to be limited to group times. As the EYFS document suggests, 'Sing about something you are doing such as "We are getting Mina ready for bed"' (DfES 2007: 111). Any tune will do, but well-known ones such as 'Here We Go Round the Mulberry Bush' or 'London's Burning' often work well.

Planning

- Plan to continually add to the setting's collection of nursery rhymes.

- Encourage all members of the setting to sing and to share their own collections.

Resourcing

(♪) Songs and rhymes appear in a variety of formats: board books, soft books and lift-the-flap books.

(♪) PEEP produces CDs of nursery rhymes and songs. They also produce a series of DVDs on how rhymes help a baby's language development.

The EYFS principles

The EYFS principles are acknowledged in this activity. It is because Suzanne knows Robert as an individual that she has decided to try action rhymes with him. She knows that at his level of physical development he is eager to move around and that he might well enjoy songs which incorporate actions. Her close relationship with him enables him to trust her when he is exposed to unfamiliar actions, and she is also able to be responsive to his interests as she has a clear idea of what he will respond to. The nursery's environment which sets aside good lengths of time for uninterrupted singing and movement in quiet places supports learning times such as these. (See 'enough time', p. 10.)

From 8–20 months

Development matters

- Move their whole bodies to sounds they enjoy, such as music or a regular beat.

Key words

positive disposition, mastery learning

Activity

Albert is eighteen months old, and he has shown a great interest in books since he was a tiny baby. He is now a very active toddler, running, climbing, sitting down and jumping up again for much of the day. His childminder, Alison, also looks after a three-year-old girl who enjoys books too and often shows Albert pictures in her books. Albert's favourite book at the moment is *Old MacDonald Has a Farm*. He particularly likes the animal sounds and the actions that go with each animal. He is an expert on which sound each animal makes and is clearly proud of his accuracy! Alison has found some farm animals and has put them ready for the song. As she sings the line 'And on that farm there was a duck', Albert picks up the duck and says 'Quack.' His concentration is held throughout, and, eventually, Alison reaches his favourite animal: the horse. When she sings 'And on that farm there was a horse', Albert jumps up and down with great enjoyment making galloping actions and making clicking sounds like the hooves of a horse.

'What a splendid horse', says Alison, 'Shall we sing "Horsey, Horsey, Don't You Stop?"'

Albert nods his head, and Alison sings through her increasing range of songs involving horses with Albert continuing to supply the actions.

Learning story

- **Emotional learning.** Albert needs the companionship of one of his important people to gain maximum satisfaction from this activity. Although Alison sometimes sees Albert turning the pages of his books quietly by himself, he will usually bring the book he has chosen to her and hold it up to show that he wants to sit close to her so that they can share the book together. Alison always respects his choice by saying, 'You want that one, do you? OK, let's sit over here', and, in this way, Albert begins to learn that he is able to make choices which are valued. (See 'key person', p. ☺ 25.) He is also learning that the sharing of songs and books satisfies the emotional need that he, and all very young children have, in gaining the close attention of people they are learning to love and trust. (See 'mastery learner', p. 9.) ☺

- **Social learning.** Babies and toddlers are always in the company of those who are caring for them, and so much of their learning can be thought of as sociable. Although Albert will look at books on his own for a little while, at his level of development it is a much less satisfying experience for him. The enjoyable processes of choosing and sharing that are a part of this type of activity are teaching him about the joys of joint discoveries of new songs and stories and the comfort provided by the well-known ones.

- **Cognitive learning.** Stories and songs teach us about our culture and form the basis of many well-known books that Albert will come across as he grows older. The activity is sufficiently enjoyable to hold his attention for the duration of the song, and, thus, he is developing a *positive disposition* towards books. (See 'positive dispositions', p. 18.) This will be a valuable attitude when he ☺ comes to learn to read later on. Through the content of the song, Alison is helping Albert to match the farm animals to the pictures on the page. By drawing his attention to the differences between how each animal looks and sounds, she is helping his discriminatory skills and his representational skills to develop.

Look, listen and note

As an experienced childminder, Alison has an effective system of observing the children in her care. She has noted Albert's preferences and has shared them with his parents. His family have also talked to Alison about the songs and rhymes that they share at home so that Albert can benefit from a widening selection of songs and books. Alison has some ideas of new songs and stories she plans to introduce to Albert and also shares these ideas with his parents.

Effective practice

It seems increasingly difficult to find calm spaces and generous lengths of time to spend singing and reading with young children, and yet these are the main requirements to building the positive attitude that children will need later to master the complexities of reading and perhaps become a creative musician or writer. The main motivation to read a book is to discover what happens on the next page, and, for a love of books to develop into a habit, young children need to be provided with time and space to engage deeply with the subject matter of the story. Books need to be a high priority for the practitioner who has the skill to choose those which are well written and illustrated and which will contain rich material to engage both child and adult.

Planning

Plan regular points in the year to review the books in stock. Throw out those beyond repair but keep or replace any still loved by individual children. Keep scouring children's bookshops for new titles.

The EYFS principles

By observing and noticing Albert's predisposition to running and climbing, Alison has respected his uniqueness by choosing action songs and stories to share with him. By using this knowledge of him she is strengthening his desire to learn, which may, in time, become a mindset that will enable him to become a mastery learner. (See 'mastery learner', p. 9.) Alison clearly ☺ enjoys these shared reading experiences, and, by showing this to Albert, he is likely to appreciate the enjoyment that reading, singing and dancing for pleasure can provide. He will also learn that he is competent in these activities. An enabling environment such as this one will provide a range of books and toys, such as the farm animals, which are likely to engage Albert's interest, and there will be enough time and quiet spaces for them to enjoy these times together without interruption.

From 16–26 months

Development matters

- Begin to move to music, listen to or join in rhymes and songs.

Key words

dancing, symbolic representation, self-expression

Activity

As it was a winter term, Josie's setting planned to provide some indoor movement activities to complement the more vigorous activities available outside. They decided to link music with movement and to introduce the children to some group sessions where some recorded music would be played for children to listen and dance to. The staff cleared the furniture from a central section of the setting and talked to the children about what was going to happen. Before the music was played, children had time to think about how a mouse might move and how an elephant might move. Josie had enjoyed watching other children pretending to be different animals but did not want to join in. When the music started, she put her hands over her ears and went into the book area to sit on the comfy cushions. She watched a large group of children noisily stamping their feet as elephants and then tiptoe silently as mice. The adults asked children to choose which animal they would like to dance to next, and, by the end of the session, they had been moving like snakes, lions, cats, birds and bees! Next, the children played a different game. They had to listen carefully to the music, and, when it stopped, sit down on the floor until the music started once more. Josie watched all this activity intently, but when her key person, Andrea, came across to her and suggested that she might like to join in, she shook her head and snuggled further into the comfy cushions. Andrea stayed with her for a while, and they talked together about the animals and the 'musical bumps' game. When everyone was tired from all the dancing, a practitioner suggested that they sit down and sing some nursery rhymes about animals.

Later on in the session, Andrea read *Kipper's Toy Box,* which had many of the animals that the children had just been thinking about. Josie sat close to Andrea as she read the story and listened closely all the way through. 'Did you like that story, Josie?' asked Andrea as she reached the last page. Josie smiled and nodded. Later, Andrea found Josie back in the book corner looking through the books about animals that the staff had selected as a link activity to the dancing and singing. The majority of the children had enjoyed the vigorous activity involved in dancing like animals and the satisfaction of singing well-known nursery rhymes about them. They had also enjoyed the way in which dancing and singing can be shared with everyone else as well as the imaginative element of pretending that, just for a while, they are not small children, but huge elephants, tiny mice, slithery snakes or gliding birds. (See 'key aspects of play', p. 15.)

Learning story

- **Emotional learning.** Often, children will need a sympathetic adult to encourage them to dance and sing, but, once they have experienced the sensation and understood that it is encouraged and valued by the setting, they will be eager to repeat it as it is a form of creativity that is accessible to them at any level of development. Josie, however, did not feel confident enough to commit herself to a large, boisterous group of dancers, and some children, although fascinated by the idea of dancing and singing, may need a quieter environment and a longer time to think through the idea before joining in. She could still be seen to benefit emotionally from the activity as she clearly enjoyed watching the spectacle and wanted to know more about the animals through quiet conversation and stories with her key person.

- **Social learning.** This kind of group activity, although not every child's favourite pastime, gives young children the opportunity to play in ways that are not entirely individual. Developmentally, at this stage, children will tend to play alongside each other but not yet be ready to join in with a cooperative venture. Dancing, and particularly singing, are exceptions as they naturally happen in small and large groups.

- **Cognitive learning.** Children are learning to listen carefully and to concentrate for long periods of time. They are learning to react with their whole bodies to changes of speed and to control their movements. Through their dancing, the children are beginning to learn about 're-presenting' experiences, that is making one thing stand for something else. In this case, they are making their bodies represent animals and birds through movement. Later on, they will continue this process by using other creative processes such as role play, painting and writing to represent a wide range of experiences. (See 'making connections', p. 6.)

Look, listen and note

- Practitioners will observe not only children's, such as Josie's, responses, but also the enjoyment that most of the children will have experienced and think of ways to enable small groups of children to dance and sing together without adults being present.

- By providing instruments and enough space for dancing to happen on a regular basis, children will be free to choose and engage in the activity themselves.

- Information can be usefully shared with parents so that they, too, can encourage children's self-expression through dance and singing at home and be clearer as to the cognitive, creative and emotional benefits these activities offer. (See 'activities and provision', p. 17.)

Effective practice

- As well as understanding the value that creative music and movement offer, it will not become a reality unless there is sufficient space for children to move freely.

- Time will need to be set aside and sessions planned into the curriculum. (See 'enough time', p. 10.)

- Some simple props such as scarves and instruments will encourage children to dance, and simple costumes such as masks will spark children's imaginations.

Planning

Plan for both structured movement sessions (these can be informal, perhaps, in the outdoor area) and ongoing provision to encourage children to incorporate movement and singing into their ordinary play.

The EYFS principles

Josie's individuality and uniqueness is respected here as she is clearly not going to enjoy joining in a large-scale cooperative session such as this. Her particular learning style of quiet reflection and enjoyment of stories is valued by the setting as Andrea does not try to jolly her along but sits with her and helps her to learn about animals through her individual style of learning. Staff respect the fact that, for Josie, dancing may happen rather later on, or she may find that performing is not one of her preferred methods of self-expression. The responsiveness that Andrea shows to Josie's attitude is evidence of a reflective setting in which relationships are sensitive and where children's preferences are valued. An enabling setting will provide alternative ways for children to learn and will have thought about the range of children's temperaments which may mean that they will not all wish to join in a large and possibly noisy activity.

From 22–36 months

Development matters

- Create sounds by banging, shaking, tapping or blowing.

Key words
rhythm, musical compositions

Activity

In an inner-city nursery school, staff planned to increase children's awareness of music and to encourage them to listen to music and to create their
own. To reflect the cultural diversity of the area, one of the practitioners,
Debbie, had found a local shop selling inexpensive musical instruments
from around the world. She had bought some shakers made from seed
heads and some wooden instruments which made interesting sounds when
tapped or scraped with a beater. The staff decided to show the new instruments to the children during small group times so that they had an opportunity to teach children how to use and care for the instruments before
putting them in the music area for the children to use independently. To
start the session, Debbie played what she called a 'question and answer'
game with her small group. She clapped her hands in a simple rhythm and
asked the children to repeat it by clapping the same rhythm. The most
popular rhythms were the staff's and children's first names. After much
practice, many of the children became expert at this, and so Debbie asked
one or two of them to make up a rhythm that the rest of the group could
copy. After yet more practice, she handed a shaker to one child who she
had seen was enjoying the game and asked him to make up a rhythm with a
shaker. He made the three syllables of his name, 'Timothy', and Debbie
clapped the rhythm back to him. Soon, several other children joined in with
the game. This 'clapping game' as it was soon called, became very popular
with the children, who played it with a partner or in small groups in the
music area either with shakers and bangers or just by clapping their hands.
Debbie and the other staff searched through their stock of rhymes and songs
and added the ones that had a particularly strong rhythmic beat to the music
area such as 'Humpty Dumpty' and 'One, Two, Buckle My Shoe.' Later,
they began to add stories which also had a strong rhythm such as *Room on
the Broom*.

Learning story

- **Emotional learning.** Many young children have a real affinity with
  rhythm, which may derive from before birth when they were in
  close proximity to their mother's rhythmic heartbeat. As small babies
  they may have been soothed by being gently rocked to sleep or by

being carried in slings by their parents and carers. Songs and rhymes with a strong beat attract their attention and can provide a deep emotional satisfaction and sense of enjoyment.

- **Social learning.** Although children will respond to music and rhythms on their own, it is very often as a small group activity that this kind of learning is most effective. Children will seek out others who they know enjoy the same songs and rhymes, and sometimes these shared times will be the beginning of friendships that are enduring as they are based on shared interests.

- **Cognitive learning.** Children's listening, discriminating and memory skills are developed by activities such as these, and they also learn about turn-taking and the beginnings of the skills associated with performance such as starting and stopping together. They will learn about a range of instruments from different cultures and traditions and how to care for and preserve delicate objects. Their coordination will benefit from learning how to make sounds accurately from instruments, and, as they create more complex combinations of sounds, they may develop increased confidence in their ability to create musical compositions.

Look, listen and note

- As well as observing and noting individual children's interest in music, this is an area that requires constant monitoring to ensure that it is attractive to use and that the instruments are in good condition and being used appropriately.

- Consider and plan how children's learning can be progressed as it will become apparent that all levels of ability are present in the music area! (See 'rich environment', p. 7.)

Effective practice

- To ensure that there are challenging opportunities for all levels of ability, practitioners may consider adding some pitched instruments such as thumb harps, a glockenspiel or a range of bells.

- Children can be encouraged to compose their own music, recording it either by their own marks of notation or on to a tape or CD.

Planning

- Plan for small-group clapping activities and bring instruments into group time to demonstrate their use.

- Plan also for children's independent use by making an attractive music area with instruments and books containing rhymes and songs.

Resourcing

- xylophone
- chime bars
- wooden blocks
- drum
- cymbals
- triangles
- shakers
- sand blocks
- castanets
- rain sticks

- whistles

- recorders

Donaldson, Juliet and Scheffler, Alex (2001) *Room on the Broom,* Basingstoke: Macmillan.

The EYFS principles

Musical experiences for young children reinforce the notion of them as competent learners. Most children will respond eagerly to actions such as clapping, beating or shaking and will gain great satisfaction from their achievements. As it is a physical activity, most children will enjoy a considerable level of success and even those who the adults feel may not show an aptitude for keeping in time will benefit from the 'joining in' aspect of music-making. If a music area is set up for children to use independently as and when they wish, their individuality is respected and their autonomy is given the opportunity to develop. Adults can sometimes lead and sometimes join a music session, but there should be planning to allow children to use it freely. An enabling music environment will provide for music and dancing as a regularly available activity. It is advisable to start with a few bangers and shakers and gradually to introduce other instruments from a range of cultures – finally introducing a pitched instrument. (See 'mastery learner', p. 9 and 'activities and provision', p. 17.)

From 30–50 months

Development matters

- Explore and learn how sounds can be changed.

Activity

During a very wet summer, Sam's nursery staff had introduced a few 'rainy activities'. Nearly every day there were big clouds in the sky, and staff and some children had made 'Incey Wincey Spider' and his web in the creative area. These they had placed in a sheltered position in the nursery garden. Very regularly, it seemed, 'down came the rain and washed the spider out', and he had to be replaced in his web in the hopes that the sun would dry him out! One day, some children were drawing the grey clouds with crayons by looking at the reflections of the clouds in a mirror which a practitioner was holding as it lay on a table in the garden. Suddenly, down came great splashes of rain, and everyone rushed to collect up the toys that were

Choosing a drum from the music area

outside. Once inside, Jim, one of the staff, said, 'Listen, children, can you hear the rain on the roof?'

The children listened intently as the rain splashed down above their heads, and Jim began drumming the sound of the rain with his fingers on a table. Soon the children joined in and continued for a while, until Jim said, 'Sshh, listen, I think the rain is stopping.' He then developed this listening game into a dramatic story which included the soft sounds of the start of a rainstorm. This was followed by increasing volume as the 'rain' increased, and then Sam suggested some thunder.

He chose a drum from the music area to create the thunder, and the shape of the storm developed with other children adding ideas such as a soft wind, then a gale and finally the sun at the end of the storm. Staff noticed that this game was often repeated by the children in their role play in the following days and weeks and, as a result of the children's continued interest, added some 'rainy props' to the role-play area such as boots, a small child's umbrella and some rain capes. Subsequently, they noticed how many variations there were to the imaginary rain game, with any number of cats, giants and babies being left out in the rain and needing to be rescued! (See 'adult's role', p. 21.)

Learning story

- **Emotional learning.** Children are able to make an immediate response to something that they have just experienced. This is meaningful to young children whose most effective learning happens when an experience is current or very recent.

  The children in the group could easily identify with the theme of the storm as it was familiar to all of them, and their subsequent imaginative role play reflected the powerful impression that recent storms had made on them. Sometimes children are made anxious by storms, especially those involving thunder and so can benefit from playing out their fears in a safe way such as this. (See 'key aspects of play', p. 15.)

- **Social learning.** The early years setting is a good place for a child to discover that other children have similar anxieties to them and that staff are aware of these. To be able to play out recent situations with friends is a richly creative experience, and role play in particular gives children the opportunity to assign roles, invent a script and control the direction of the play.

- **Cognitive learning.** In this instance, the practitioners decided to use the rainstorm as a creative inspiration, and so it was not used at this time to help children understand about scientific aspects such as properties of water. That might well follow at a later date. What children were learning from this activity was how to interpret, or 're-present', something that happens in real life in a creative and imaginative way. This helps the experience to become internalised and under children's control so that they can think and talk about it in rational and dispassionate ways. Here they are learning to match what they see, hear, feel and think to sounds and movements that they can make; the beginnings of genuine creativity. (See 'making connections', p. 6.)

Look, listen and note

As well as observing individual children's responses to everyday and more unusual events, staff here have considered how best to provide for them to recreate these events by music and role play. They may extend these opportunities by suggesting that children could draw or paint their impressions of rainstorms and continue to share stories, pictures and rhymes that explore this theme. Careful monitoring of these activities and provision, together with staff discussion, will reveal what the children are learning creatively, cognitively and emotionally.

Effective practice

- By widening the range of artefacts, based on the theme of rain, that they show to children, practitioners will be deepening their understanding of how rain has been represented by artists in the past and the possibilities that are open to them.

- Discussions about the beauty of nature can lead to a debate about our responsibility to care for the natural world and the challenges that threaten it. (See 'skills and attitudes of creativity', p. 21.) ☺

Planning

- It may not be possible to pre-plan an event such as this in the accepted sense as the situation is one that happened spontaneously.

- After the event, there will need to be planning to continue the children's interest in a formative and productive way.

Resourcing

Provide materials to support children's recreation of the event and associated ideas. These would include role play, small-world play, music, stories and rhymes.

The EYFS principles

Staff in this setting are demonstrating an awareness of children's individual sensitivities by acknowledging the range of emotions that the storms seem to have stirred up in the children. They have provided opportunities for children to address their feelings by helping them to express them creatively and to take control of them. The setting is enabling in its attitude as well by being flexible enough to set up immediate opportunities to recreate the rainstorm and to change the role-play area to accommodate children's changing interests. By making this provision, they are helping children not only to become creative but also to become stronger and more competent as they discover creativity as a possible outlet to channel the strong feelings that are often attached to new experiences.

From 30–50 months

Development matters

- Imitate and create movement in response to music.

Activity

Allanah is nearly four and comes from a large, close family who enjoy meeting together regularly. Often, towards the end of a meal, some musical instruments will appear, and she will watch as her older relatives start to sing and dance in time to the music. Sometimes she is allowed to join in too, and she feels very special as she swirls around following the mood of the music – sometimes fast and exciting and sometimes sad and slow. At her setting, practitioners had invited two musicians, a flautist and a keyboard player to spend a session playing for the children. Many of the children had not seen musical instruments before and were curious as the musicians let them feel the shiny flute and run their fingers over the black and white notes of the keyboard. Then the musicians made some sounds on their instruments, and some of the children were not expecting the sounds to be so loud. The musicians played high notes, low notes, loud notes and soft notes and asked the children which they liked the best. Then they began to play some music, soft and gentle at first but then getting faster and louder. Grace, Allanah's key person, noted how excited Allanah looked as the music began and she started to clap her hands and sway to and fro in time to the rhythms. She asked her if she had heard music like it before, and Allanah said 'Yes, at home.' Soon the musicians suggested that some children might like to dance to their music, and a few, including Allanah, jumped up, eager to join in. As the music progressed, it became clear to the practitioners that Allanah was skilled at dancing and that she was enjoying demonstrating her expertise. Many of the children sat and watched the musicians and dancers rather than joining in but all were interested and engaged regardless of whether they took part. As the music ended, the musicians asked the children if they would like to make some notes on the instruments, and some of the children who had watched the dancing were keen to try to make some sounds. Allanah, however, did not want to join that activity and went to sit quietly in the role-play area gently rocking a doll and singing it a lullaby.

Learning story

- **Emotional learning.** This activity has great significance for Allanah. She is a rather shy child from a family which is in a cultural minority in the area, and she has not always felt that she belongs to the setting in the way that most of the other children do. For her to experience the joy of movement at her setting not only gives her an outlet for her emotions but enables her to feel at home with an activity that is important to her and at which she excels. (See 'adult's role', p. 21.)

- **Social learning.** As we can see from Allanah's family, music and dance are strong identifying and unifying forces. Music and dance define people culturally, and many groups of people have taken their traditional music with them when they have travelled from their homelands. Very young children identify themselves by the songs and music that they are familiar with, and the opportunity that a setting offers to reinforce these identities helps children to feel that they belong and that their culture is valued.

- **Cognitive learning.** A sophisticated range of learning is encased within this musical session. As well as the creative experience of appreciating live music, children have the opportunity to create an individual dance routine by matching the mood, tempo and volume of the music to their movements. They can also learn about trying to making musical sounds, which is a demanding physical activity requiring good coordination, sometimes great strength and often accurate breath control. Children's knowledge of different cultures will be much enhanced by experiences such as these and can be followed up by learning songs and rhymes during group times which may be unfamiliar to them.

Look, listen and note

Observe individual levels of children's development so that practitioners can help to move each child's learning forward. Note children's individual response to musical activities to ensure that challenging experiences are available for children at all levels of ability.

Effective practice

- Provide an interesting range of instruments for children to experience.

- Provide time and appropriate spaces for music and dance.

- Consider ways of enabling children with visual and hearing impairments to have access to music-making and dance.

- Read stories about music, put posters about music or dance up in the setting and encourage the inclusion of music and dance in role play.

Planning

- Plan to have visiting musicians to demonstrate their skills and plan to incorporate a musical theme within topics.

- Plan games such as 'What's that sound?' to develop children's listening skills and plan movement sessions where children respond to preset sounds.

The EYFS principles

By inviting the musicians into the setting, staff have demonstrated their understanding of music as a valuable creative force that often helps children to express themselves in unique ways. By encouraging this kind of self-expression, staff enable children to grow in self-confidence and to demonstrate that they have talents that might otherwise go unnoticed. Staff at this setting are aware of the different creative traditions in children's families and are keen to build music into their planning as one way of making links with families from different cultures. An enabling environment will work at contacting artists and musicians prepared to work with young children and to plan follow-up activities to help sustain children's interest.

From 40–60 months

Development matters

- Begin to build a repertoire of songs and dances.

Activity

Staff at a busy early excellence centre have been planning to help children make choices and to begin to think critically about the choices they make. It has been decided that, to help children with this process, staff will encourage children to make choices about which their favourite songs and rhymes are and then to say why they like them. Having made their selection, staff helped the children to make a collection of their best-loved songs and rhymes and put the collection in the music area so that children could access them at any time. They began at small group times and individually asked children which songs they enjoyed most. The staff gradually encouraged a culture of children being able to articulate why they enjoyed some songs more than others. Some children replied that they liked a song because they sang it at home, while some enjoyed the beat or the tune. Others enjoyed the sounds or the actions that accompanied the song, and some liked the picture that accompanied the song in the nursery-rhyme book. Children were then asked to illustrate their favourite song or to dictate a phrase, such as 'Darren likes it when the Grand Old Duke marches up the hill', and practitioners scribed the children's views and added the songs to children's illustrations or comments. When the collection was substantial, the pages were fastened together, and the book was placed in the music area.

Two children who did not take any interest in the songbook were Chesna and Jaromil. They were a brother and sister who had recently joined the centre, having moved with their family to the area from their former home in Eastern Europe. Practitioners asked their mother for some best-loved songs from their family to be added to the music book, and, when this happened, staff saw big smiles from the two children as they tried to teach everyone their special songs. (See 'skills and attitudes of creativity', p. 21 and 'activities and provision', p. 17.)

Learning story

- **Emotional learning.** This activity is about empowering children to be selective and to follow up their choices with reasons. The children's choices are then valued as the staff make them up into a book which is placed alongside other nursery-rhyme books for children to use in the music area.

   For Chesna and Jaromil in particular, the experience of being included in this type of activity helps them in the process of feeling that they belong to this new community and that they have something of value to offer which will be enjoyed by other children. (See 'adult's role', p. 21.)

- **Social learning.** The experience of making a group book, whether it is a music book or a storybook, helps all children to derive satisfaction from being a part of a cooperative venture. A group project such as this is much more effective as a learning experience than it would have been if just one child had expressed a view about a song, and the fact that many of the children took part meant that much language development took place as they debated their choices amongst themselves and with practitioners.

- **Cognitive learning.** Children here are being encouraged to make reasoned choices, to be articulate about their choices and to debate them with others. They are learning that their views and ideas can be rational and that others will listen to thoughtful discussion. They will learn that their views and opinions will not necessarily be the same as other people's. This particular discovery begins the process of the development of 'theory of mind' where children learn about the possibility of a wide range of values and beliefs and learn to respect others' viewpoints.

Look, listen and note

- This is an activity that practitioners can use to discover the breadth of individual children's musical experiences. Some children will have come to the setting with a deep knowledge of nursery rhymes whilst for others singing and saying rhymes may be new.

- Music is a good area to use for the beginnings of making choices as there are no right and wrong answers, and children's genuine choices can be respected. (See 'right and wrong answers', p. 15.)

Effective practice

- To ensure that children use the music book, staff will need to ensure that the book is added to so that each child who wishes to have a song or rhyme included has that chance.

- The book will need to be sturdy and often checked as over-use may well lead to its disintegration!

- The music area will need to be available for long periods of uninterrupted time and to be well maintained so that it is attractive to use with enough instruments in good working order. (See 'enough time', p. 10 and 'rich environment', p. 11.) ©

Planning

- Plan to spend time seeking out children's preferences and scribing them in the songbook.

- Plan a music area that is attractive and large enough to accommodate several children comfortably and plan to have an adult 'drop in' to model the use of the area.

Resourcing

- An attractive table displaying a range of instruments in good condition.

- Collections of songbooks plus children's own.

- Paper and pencils for children to use to compose their own songs and music.

- Some examples of written music for children to see that there are different forms of writing.

Music, 'a different form of writing'

The EYFS principles

Children are helped to be strong and competent by having their opinions sought and valued. The recognition that each child may have a different reason for the choice they have made reinforces the concept that children are unique. Staff who respect this variety by not expecting uniformity are demonstrating that they have a true understanding of the notion of positive relationships. The action of displaying the children's work as a book for everyone's use in the music area reflects an environment that enables children to feel that their individual ideas and preferences are important and have value.

Developing imagination and imaginative play

From birth–11 months

Development matters

- Smile with the pleasure of recognisable playthings.

Key words
transitional objects, well-being

Activity

Tommy lives in a second-floor flat in South London. There is a very large tree just outside his bedroom window. In the tree, a blackbird sings nearly every morning, especially in the spring, and Tommy's parents have seen him turn his head to listen to the blackbird's song. They talked about this to Tommy's child-minder, Jackie, who cares for him every weekday. They tell Jackie that they have found a soft toy that looked rather like a blackbird in a local shop that sings when pressed in the middle; they bought it, and it has become one of Tommy's favourite toys. Jackie asks if Tommy can bring the soft toy with him when he comes to her house, and she then plays with Tommy, showing him how to squeeze the bird to make the sound. Even though Tommy, at nine months, cannot accurately squeeze the toy to make it sing, it soon goes everywhere with him, and he looks for it, particularly when it is time for his daytime sleep, to take with him into his cot. When Tommy is playing, he repeatedly holds out the blackbird toy for Jackie to squeeze, and he smiles with pleasure when he hears the sound it makes. Sometimes Jackie plays 'peep-bo' with the toy, making it disappear and appear behind a muslin cloth and sometimes she sings 'Sing a Song of Sixpence' and pretends that the blackbird 'pecks' Tommy's nose.

Learning story

- **Emotional learning.** Tommy is comforted by what is sometimes called a 'transitional object', that is something that helps very young children to make the link between the familiar setting of the home and the less familiar setting of the childminder. Particularly at sleep-time he is soothed by the connection the blackbird toy makes between his two cots in his two bedrooms. Although probably not yet able to make a connection between the sound of the toy and the blackbird's song, the presence of the toy nevertheless provides Tommy with an assurance of safety, security and well-being.

- **Social learning.** The shared interest that both his parents and his childminder have shown in his favourite toy give Tommy the under-standing that what matters to him is also of interest to those people who are most important to him. The shared games, together with the delight that both his parents and Jackie demonstrate when playing with him and the blackbird toy, teach Tommy that enjoying playing together with others is valuable and enriching. He begins to learn that he can get more satisfaction and enjoyment from his toy by sharing it with others.

- **Cognitive learning.** Tommy is learning through these shared experiences with his key people that what he enjoys and finds interesting other people will enjoy too. He is learning that toys can be used as props, to make sounds and to appear and disappear. The 'peep-bo' game, in particular, is valuable at this stage of development as young babies need to understand about the normal comings and goings of everyday life. To be able to practise coming and going in a safe, playful way reassures them that when people go away they come back again.

Look, listen and note

A knowledge of individual children's preferences helps the very youngest babies feel safe in a setting that is not their home. For these children, it is particularly important for practitioners to build on routines that have been established at home, as continuity is of the essence in maintaining a baby's feelings of security and trust. They will feel loved if what arouses their curiosity is respected and if time is given to a genuine sharing of their interests. Noting down a baby's particular interests or favourite toys will be valuable information in settings where practitioners work in shifts and can be helpful in informing parents too.

Effective practice

- With young babies, the key to effective practice is to have time to listen to them, time to be with them and time to share enjoyable experiences with them.

- It matters less what practitioners 'do' with babies than how they do it. At this stage of their development, 'being' is more important that 'doing.'

- Shared times playing games with favourite toys, singing and looking at books and enjoying each other's company is the most effective good practice.

Planning

- The most important thing to plan for is time. Young babies will smile with the pleasure of a recognisable plaything when they are relaxed and in the company of someone that they trust and love.

- Babies often have one or more playthings that mean a lot to them and provide added security. Planning to use these in songs and stories reinforces the responsiveness of the practitioner. (See 'key person', p. 10.)

Resourcing

- A range of soft toys or dolls which are always nearby for a baby to become familiar with.

- Cosy, quiet spaces for practitioners and babies to play and sing together.

The EYFS principles

Tommy is being helped to become a strong and self-confident individual because his parents are giving some time to consider what is important to him and to share these things with Jackie, who is also responsible for his everyday care. This liaison is vital as it provides the continuity of emotional experience that Tommy needs at his stage of life when he has to be in different places and cared for by different people. The adults' relationships are clearly positive as his carers respect and trust each other and are eager to take up suggestions that will benefit Tommy. His two environments both support his development as they have given time and effort to playing with him in ways that he will value.

From 8–20 months

Development matters

- Enjoy making noises or movements spontaneously.

Key words
trust, belonging, imagine

Activity

Janice, who is eighteen months old, has begun to attend an early excellence centre in the nearest town to the village where she lives. Her mother drops her off on her way to work three days a week. Staff have been trying to help Janice settle as she has found the transition between home and setting a difficult one to make and is normally rather withdrawn. Her mother is usually in a rush to get to work on time, and there hasn't been a lot of time for staff to find out about what Janice is interested in. One day, Gill, her key person, is sharing a book with her about farm animals, and when she reaches the page with the horses, Janice looks up at her and smiles.

'Do you like horses, Janice?' asks Gill, and she makes the sound of horses' hooves with her tongue. Janice jumps up and tries to make the same sound. Gill decides to leave the farm story and sing some songs about horses with Janice. She sings 'Horsey, Horsey' and then 'This Is the Way the Ladies Ride', bouncing Janice carefully on her knee before letting her slide gently 'down into the ditch'. Janice climbs up on Gill's knee and says, 'Again.' This is the first time that Janice has seemed to relax and really enjoy a shared activity in the six weeks that she has been attending the setting. Gill shares this news with other staff members with considerable relief. When her mother comes to fetch Janice, Gill tells her about Janice's interest in horses.

'Yes', says her mother, 'Well, we keep horses, and Janice helps me feed them most days before we leave home.'

The next day that Janice was due into the setting, staff sorted out some horses from the farm animal set, and Gill used them in her play with Janice. As she played with her, Gill talked to Janice about her horses at home, and Janice made more clicking sounds and was clearly enjoying this companionable play.

Learning story

- **Emotional learning.** Janice was rather a shy child and found the contrast between the busy setting and her quiet village cottage quite overwhelming. Her love of the horses that she and her mother cared for each day was an important part of her life, and to have that recognised by her key person has enabled her to feel that she belongs to this new place which, up until now, had seemed to have little in common with her home life. Not only does she now feel valued as her interest has been discovered but she also begins to trust Gill who has shown that she cares about her and will enjoy sharing Janice's interest with her. (See 'adult's role', p. 21.)

- **Social learning.** Janice's new found self-confidence will help her to begin to enjoy other aspects of life in the setting. She now feels that she belongs here and that she can trust the adults who care for her. So she will be able to engage more fully with other areas in the setting and begin to express her views and feelings in what she now understands to be a place where she can more confidently explore, play and make friends.

- **Cognitive learning.** Small-world play can help young children recognise that their interests, such as horses, can be represented by lifelike replicas. Using one thing to represent another is a significant cognitive step and allows children to develop their play by using their imagination to develop pretend scenarios. At first, the model horses may just be put in fields and taken out again, but, as Janice's powers of invention are encouraged, she is likely to invent ever more complex games and add spoken language such as animal sounds and instructions to the horses to enhance her play scripts. (See 'rich environment', p. 11 and 'spiral curriculum', p. 14.)

Look, listen and note

A set of observations will help practitioners decide how best to help children, such as Janice, to feel that they belong to the setting. As part of every setting's commitment to the EYFS and to 'Every Child Matters', there is an onus on practitioners to help children towards feelings of engagement and belonging which are key to all areas of development and to successful learning. Earlier and more effective liaison with Janice's mother, or perhaps a home visit, would probably have given useful information about their life in the country with their horses and may have given some valuable clues as to how staff could help Janice feel more at home.

Effective practice

- Ensuring a good range of small-world toys as well as a wide range of dolls representing different educational and physical needs and different beliefs and cultures help children to identify with the setting and to feel that they belong.

- A wide range of these toys also helps to develop children's imaginative skills as long as they are presented in imaginative ways and children are able to use them flexibly and for long periods of time so as to fully engage with the plots they devise. (See 'rich environment', p. 11 and 'enough time', p. 10.)

Planning

Effective planning, in this case, has been based on evidence gathered from observing Janice's play and recognising her interest in horses. This knowledge gives practitioners a 'key' to engaging Janice and they will find pictures, stories and songs that interest her.

Resourcing

It is important to encourage parents and carers to bring in photos and other artefacts from home supporting the children's interests. This will help them develop a sense of trust and belonging.

The EYFS principles

The setting have worked hard to help Janice to move towards being resilient and capable. Transition from home to setting had challenged her view of herself as competent as she found few similarities between life here and life as she had experienced it at home. Her naturally quiet personality held her back from forming relationships outside her home, and, as a result, she needed a boost to her self-esteem to build up her view of herself as lovable and competent. This was achieved by Gill's professional attitude and by her understanding of the importance of forming the emotional attachment that Janice needed. The environment has shown sensitivity to Janice's fragile self-concept by devoting time and effort to making that first significant step and by helping her feel that the setting was a place where she could feel at home.

From 16–26 months

Development matters

- Pretend that one object represents another, especially when objects have characteristics in common.

Key words

imaginative play, innovative thinking

Activity

Luke, who is two years old, lives with his mother, her partner and an older sister who is four. He attends a nursery which is attached to the hospital where his parents both work. At nursery, one of his favourite types of play is with the dolls and cradles. He spends a lot of time putting not only dolls but also toy animals into the cradles, kissing each one carefully. He then takes off the covers and lifts them out again, saying 'Hi-ya' to each one before aiming feeding bottles in the direction of their mouths. He enjoys covering the dolls and toys with a blanket and rocking them to and fro in his arms. He is especially delighted if his key person sings 'Hush-a-Bye Baby' whilst the babies are being rocked to sleep.

Learning story

- **Emotional learning.** Luke is probably copying the caring behaviour that he has seen his sister use in her play and may also be
demonstrating that he has absorbed the culture of caring that is a
part of his family's everyday life.

  He is a gentle child who clearly gains some emotional satisfaction
from acting as the carer or parent to others. The fact that the staff
support him in his caring actions help him to feel that he is valued
as a gentle male and they are validating aspects of his personality
which may be challenged in the future when he encounters rather
more boisterous boys in his setting. He has a well-developed
sense of imagination and is showing a high level of emotional
literacy. These two aspects of his personality will enable him to
be empathetic to others around him and to understand others'
needs and points of view.

- **Social learning.** Luke may well be popular in a social setting such as
the nursery as he is quickly aware of others' needs. His active imagination will enable him to invent rich role-play scenarios, and his
interpersonal skills will draw other children to want to play with him.
He is likely not to dominate imaginative play but to find roles for
other children and to weave ever more complex storylines together
as his imaginative skills develop. (See 'spiral curriculum', p. 14.) ⓒ

- **Cognitive learning.** This type of play, where children play 'Let's
pretend' or 'What if' games, has a range of learning purposes.
Through such games, children can do things that they cannot do
in real life and so can experience how it might feel to boil the
kettle, drive the car or rock the baby to sleep. This is, in effect, an
opportunity to practise or rehearse what may be experienced for
real in later life. (See 'key aspects of play', p. 15.) Another pur- ⓒ
pose of pretend play is to re-present, or go though again, experiences that children have already had but have not finished
processing yet. The child who has been to hospital, for example,
may have been worried by the experience and may need to act it
out again and again in a safe environment before being able to
internalise it and feel comfortable with it. This is rather like the role
play that adults sometimes go through after a traumatic experience

and which, in some circumstances, helps them to come to terms with what has happened. Sometimes imaginative play is pure fantasy where children have the freedom to be in different places from their everyday world, to do different things and to be different people. This type of imaginative play is well supported by children's storybooks such as *Time to Get Out of the Bath, Shirley* and *Where the Wild Things Are,* which reflect children's abilities to drift off into extraordinary flights of fancy.

Look, listen and note

- Regular observations of Luke's preferred types of play may lead staff to talk these through with his family to gain more information about how to best support him in his learning. They may discover, through observations, that Luke finds large group times challenging or that he has not got quite enough strategies to be assertive on occasions when he wants to play with a particular toy.

- Listening to the imaginative scenarios that he invents will inform staff of any props that may be needed.

- Noting the areas of Luke's strengths and possible difficulties will enable staff to ensure that these are catered for in the setting's planning.

Effective practice

- Providing stories and songs to complement Luke's games will enrich them further.

- Valuing his empathetic nature and supporting his gentleness on a daily basis will encourage the development of these attributes.

- The recognition of his imaginative skills will help Luke to become a mastery learner and a child who can think 'outside the box.' (See 'mastery learner', p. 9 and 'skills and attitudes of creativity', p. 21.)

Planning

- The planning here is based on observational evidence of the individual's personality, their strengths and what they may find challenging.

- Access to a key person is essential when help is needed in being inventive or when work is being done in a large group.

- Plan to acknowledge and value gentle caring personalities and to provide support for imaginative games.

Resourcing

- Resource the sand, water, small construction, role play and music areas with a range of objects that engage children's interest and encourage their imaginative skills.

- Burningham, J. (1994) *Time to Get Out of the Bath, Shirley,* London: Red Fox.

- Sendak, M. (1967) *Where the Wild Things Are,* London: Bodley Head.

The EYFS principles

By respecting a child's individuality, particularly if they show attitudes that seem different from those that many other children have, this setting is empowering Luke to learn in ways that are effective for him. Often children need to watch, listen, reflect and be calm, and yet, in an increasingly busy world, these quieter moments get squeezed out in an anxiety to 'do' and to 'achieve'. (See 'down time', p. 13.)

In fact, achieving is often accomplished much more successfully if some contemplation and thoughtfulness is built into the process, and, by valuing Luke's imaginative play, practitioners are encouraging his powers of innovative thinking to develop.

From 22–36 months

Development matters

- Begin to make believe by pretending.

Key words

inventive play, complex scenarios

Activity

Matthew's independent early years setting, Riverside, sits, as its name suggests, on the banks of a large river, which runs through the centre of the city where he lives. He sees the river every day, and he and his mother and baby brother often stop to feed the ducks on the way home. At just three, he has developed a fascination for all things 'watery' and has started attending swimming sessions at the local swimming pool at the weekends. His setting has noticed how much Matthew loves playing with the small-world ducks and how long he spent gazing at the goldfish in the tank in the entrance hall. They decide to encourage this interest by extending their supply of small-world toys with a connection to water and have bought a wooden whale and a penguin. This led staff to sort through their stories, and they found several that were set in cold, watery places which they hoped might encourage children to make links between their imaginative play and books. (See 'key aspects of play', p. 15.) They put them on prominent display and were delighted when a dad came into the setting, noticed the books and suggested to staff that he could make a scene that he called Ice World out of materials left over from framing a picture.

A few days later, Ice World arrived. It consisted of a flat piece of white plastic covered polystyrene sheet with slots in which were placed an ice mountain and an ice cave. Footprints had been made in the base which fitted those of the toy polar bear that the setting already had. Staff placed Ice World on a table at child height and put the whale, penguin and polar bear in the cave. Matthew, and many other children, were excited by this addition to their props, and staff observed that there was genuinely inventive play taking place with children using variations of stories they already knew as a basis for ever more complex scenarios. (See 'adult's role', p. 21.)

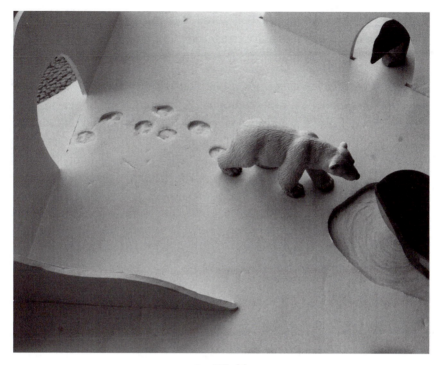

Ice World

Learning story

- **Emotional learning.** Staff here have thoughtfully built on Matthew's interests to help him to learn at a deeper level. His positive disposition, or motivation, has been increased by the steps that staff have taken, and, as the originator of the 'watery' play, Matthew feels that his ideas are important to others. Through this imaginative play, he is able to pretend that he is in an icy place and to feel what it might be like. As he creates possible stories, he may experience the emotions that are associated with his stories such as being lost in such a place and then being found, together with the fear and relief that such experiences bring with them. (See 'key aspects of play', p. 15.)

- **Social learning.** Matthew has other children to join in his play with him. He will need to learn social skills such as negotiating roles and who determines the script of the game. He will have the support of adults whom he knows well and trusts to support him as he goes through these processes, and these same adults will help him reflect on his play by asking him open questions about it.

- **Cognitive learning.** These types of imaginative play are not intended to culminate in an end product which can be quantified. Rather, 'they become a reservoir of experiences to be called on for story-telling, poetry making, in literature and drama' (Bruce 2004: 118). Cognitively, the Ice World play will have made connections in Matthew's brain which will probably lead to other activities based on the idea of ice and snow. These ideas may be represented, for example, by conversations, stories, paintings, dramatic role play or modelling and are creative ways to explore these new ideas.

Look, listen and note

By observing and discussing Matthew's interest, staff have been able to capitalise on some genuine child-initiated ideas. (See 'key aspects of play', p. 15.) These ideas are those most likely to hold children's attention for a long period of time and to motivate them to explore more deeply. This is not to say that adults should not introduce ideas to be explored in settings, but those that are more likely to lead to in-depth learning are usually those which have come from inside children's heads rather than those that have come from the adults. The sharing of the ice-world books with parents enabled one father to make a valuable contribution to the provision in the setting, and wise practitioners value families' contributions to their resources in this way.

Effective practice

- Having noted the interest of children, effective practitioners will recognise the value and importance of child-initiated learning.

- By adding to their resources of small-world animals, they have supported children's continued learning. They will then plan how children can extend their play on this theme in other areas of the setting such as the role-play and painting area and in stories. (See 'adult's role', p. 21.)

Planning

- Plan to share ideas and topics with parents and to utilise any help that they might offer or expertise they might have.

- Plan to widen children's interests across all areas of the setting using role play, graphics, paint, music and stories, where appropriate.

Resourcing

Encourage pretend play by having a wide range of easily accessible props, costumes and multi-purpose toys to stimulate children's imagination.

The EYFS principles

Responsive staff have valued Matthew's ideas by encouraging him to extend his play about things which interest him. One child's particular interest will often capture the imagination of other children too and, in this case, parents as well! When this happens, child-initiated ideas can provide opportunities for many children to get involved. This enhances Matthew's feelings of self-esteem.

The setting has encouraged parental involvement and has provided books, rhymes, songs and other activities to enable children to learn at a greater depth about things which have engaged their interest. This attitude of support will help children to develop attitudes of learning such as concentration and enthusiasm and skills of observation, critical thinking and discussion. (See 'adult's role', p. 21 and 'skills and attitudes of creativity', p. 21.)

From 30–50 months

Development matters

- Notice what adults do, imitating what is observed and then doing it spontaneously when the adult is not there.

- Use available resources to create props to support role play.

- Develop a repertoire of actions by putting a sequence of movements together.

Key words

independence, life skills

Activity

At a setting in a rural area, staff had remarked that a large proportion of the children arrived and were collected each day by car and that many had never travelled by train. As part of work that had been planned on the cross-curricular theme of 'From Here to There', they arranged to take a small group of the older children by train from the station in the village to a station further down the line which was in a village about ten miles away. Extra adults were able to accompany the children, and, afterwards, the trip was considered to have been a great success.

Back at the setting, and with help from the accompanying staff, the children were able to report on their journey and to talk at small-group times to the non-participating children about what they saw and did whilst at the stations and on the train. Staff then set up a railway station, which consisted of a ticket office and platform and an engine, in the role-play area, providing seating on the platform for passengers, a hat for the ticket collector, jackets for the guards, a boiler suit for the driver and tickets to be issued to passengers from the employee in the ticket office.

When the ticket office and station opened for business, however, confusion reigned! A few children wanted to travel on the train and asked for tickets to where they wanted to go, but most wanted to wear the hat and jackets, wave the station master's flag and climb on to the engine that had

Waiting for the noisy train, holding the ticket

been constructed from a large plastic barrel. Staff soon realised that a practitioner needed to be present in the role-play area to model the roles and to
demonstrate exactly how tickets are issued and what their purpose was.
In fact, a practitioner presence was necessary for the whole of the first
week that the station was in the role-play area as it became clear that there
were many roles to be understood and a rather complex procedure of
paying for and issuing tickets before passengers could go to the platform
and wait for their train. Eventually, however, the work that practitioners put
in to showing children how the station needed to be used began to provide
satisfying play for the children as they started to negotiate roles, hand over
pretend coins for tickets, make decisions about their journeys and talk to
each other about what they could see from the train windows. (See 'adult's
role', p. 21.)

Learning story

- **Emotional learning.** This type of role play, although complex in its range of roles and scripts, offers most children opportunities to make a contribution and to learn at whatever level is appropriate for them. Those new to train travel, or new to cooperative play such as this, can gain huge enjoyment and satisfaction from watching and learning how the role-play area can be used. It caters well for all the stages of creativity from the initial arousing of a child's curiosity to the desire, much later on, to take responsibility for the play and to adopt a leadership role in developing a storyline. (See 'stages of creativity', p. 12.)

- **Social learning.** Clearly this type of play is likely to benefit from the large group of children available to join in with the enthusiasm and ideas that they will bring with them to the game. There are opportunities for children to discover which aspects of their personalities may help or hinder them in joining a large-scale imaginative game such as this and to find out whether they are leaders or followers and whether they initiate ideas and are good team players. At the outset, this play needed significant adult input to ensure that it remained orderly and useful. As Bernadette Duffy says, 'The creative process is not about uninhibited self-expression'. Well-trained staff who are clear about the potential learning offered by play of this sort are an essential component in giving children the 'intellectual freedom to explore ideas' (1998: 77).

- **Cognitive learning.** The learning that these children are experiencing fits happily with the 'knowledge and understanding of the world' area of the curriculum. Increasingly, in an age when this generation will need to think carefully about conserving the world's resources, they are travelling less often by public transport. By suggesting alternatives, staff are raising awareness of global issues as well as helping children to understand the skills involved in travelling publicly – buying tickets, for example – and how to make decisions about train times and destinations. (See 'skills and attitudes of creativity', p. 21.)

Look, listen and note

Careful observations of children, in order to assess who would be likely to benefit most from this outing, will be helpful in guaranteeing the success of the venture. Those who are already confident enough to make a trip outside the setting and who are likely to be able to talk about their trip will probably benefit most and will also be able to offer the most valuable feedback to other children.

Effective practice

- Meticulous planning is essential before attempting a trip such as this. It is good practice for a member of staff to make the journey in advance and to talk to available railway staff about the planned trip.

- Ratios of adults to children need to be considered as does the staffing for those in the setting not taking part in the visit.

- Any accompanying parents need to be fully briefed as to the purpose of the trip, and both adults and children need to be instructed about safety issues connected with train travel.

- A photographic log of the journey will help jog children's memories when back in the setting, and, if these are made up into a book, children have a constant reminder of how the role play is best used.

- Staff should consider the learning opportunities as the visit progresses, from what is seen from the train window to what they do when reaching their destination. All these events will provide creative starting points for role play, painting, storytelling and model making in the following days and weeks.

Planning

As well as the planning mentioned above, plan for the children remaining in the setting to learn more about the experience of travelling by train with discussions, photographs and stories.

Resourcing

- A large area will be needed to recreate the engine, platform, chairs and ticket office together with resources for the children to make tickets and other train-related props.

- A member of staff will be needed to model the play. (See 'scaffolding' on p. 16.)

The EYFS principles

By encouraging children to widen their travelling experiences, the staff are helping them to develop skills of independence and choice. These are valuable life skills and will help children to take responsibility for the choices they make and thus to become more competent and confident. Staff have been responsive in recognising the need to present children with a wider range of opportunities for travelling, and the children have been able to explore these with adults they know well and feel safe with. The setting has worked hard to make this visit possible. It is not always easy to organise trips such as these, but they are enormously rich in learning opportunities when they are successful.

From 40–60 months

Development matters

- Introduce a storyline or narrative into their play.
- Play alongside other children who are engaged in the same theme.
- Play cooperatively as part of a group to act out a narrative.

Key words

communication, language and literacy; spontaneous learning

Activity

In the reception class of a large primary school in a suburban area, teaching staff planned to increase children's confidence to write through role play. As a response to some children noticing spiders' webs in the nursery garden at the start of the autumn term, staff read *The Very Busy Spider* at group time. One child wanted to make a spider, so an adult helped him by finding a brown paper bag which they stuffed and some pipe cleaners which were added for legs. After the children had gone home, staff constructed a spider's web like the one in the book from wool. It hung in a corner above the paint table but within children's reach. The spider was settled in the middle of the web, and staff placed a cardboard box below the web with a slit in the top. The spider then wrote a letter to the children saying that she had come to stay in the nursery for a while. She said in the letter that she did not have a name and asked if anyone could suggest one for her?

The next day, when the children arrived, there was great interest in the spider and her web, and, at group time, much discussion took place as to a suitable name. It was suggested by the teacher that all the ideas for names were written down, or scribed, and posted into the spider's post-box for the spider to choose. From that point onwards, a dialogue was established with every named communication from a child being answered by the spider. Although hard work on the part of the staff, the enthusiasm of the children was encouraging, as almost every child wanted to write or draw something to post into the box so that they would get a letter back. As the project developed, many ideas were contributed to the story of the spider. A 'spider's tea party' was held, complete with squashed fly biscuits thoughtfully provided by a parent.

Children made flies for the spider to catch in her web from a range of creative materials in the workshop area, and, in due course, many baby spiders appeared in the web which needed to be counted, drawn, painted and sung about.

Learning story

- **Emotional learning.** This project is an example of how creativity can, and must, 'involve the whole curriculum, not just the arts' (DfES 2007: card 4.2). It demonstrates how a child's idea can be built on by responsive staff and used by them as a rich resource to provide ways in which children can be encouraged to learn basic skills of writing and counting through play. There is great emotional satisfaction to be gained by children who get deeply involved in an imagined narrative and develop it for their own purposes. (See 'stages of creativity', p. 12 and 'mastery learner', p. 9.)

- As with other holistic learning experiences covering the wider curriculum, children can contribute to a project and gain from it at a developmental level appropriate to them as individuals. Playing in this way will engage children in deep-level learning which leads towards a positive disposition to learning. (See 'positive disposition', p. 18.)

- **Social learning.** Children of this age will enjoy joining with others in developing complex play stories and benefit from the challenge of negotiating whose ideas are followed up and whose are not. They will enjoy showing their creations to others at group times and benefit from the opportunity to discuss their ideas with supportive adults. Being able to share interesting events at nursery with parents and family helps children to realise that their ideas and views are valued in the wider community outside nursery and enables genuine links to be forged between home and setting.

- **Cognitive learning.** Children can watch and observe activities that other children engage in. They can contribute ideas and begin to take responsibility for the narrative. An open-ended play scenario like this one can provide many children with valuable learning at their specific 'zone of proximal development' (see 'zone of proximal development' p. 9). The spider's web becomes part of the nur- ☉ sery's *provision* whilst both adults and children will devise new *activities* as ideas arise. (See 'activities and provision', p. 17.) This ☉ offers a good balance between adult-led and child-led learning. Curricular learning opportunities include:

- communication, language and literacy: mark-making, writing, story-making, acting;
- maths: counting spiders and flies, cooking and eating biscuits, numbers of legs on a spider;
- knowledge and understanding of the world: the lifecycle of spiders, care of living creatures.

Look, listen and note

- Because this is an open-ended topic, specific learning outcomes may not have been possible to predict. In fact, as with much of young children's learning, they do not learn what we may have intended, but they are, nevertheless, learning something worthwhile! This is why careful observation is the key to effective assessment.

- By observing children learning as they go about their play – writing letters to the spider, painting pictures of her, counting her babies and so on, staff can make accurate notes of what is being learned and by whom.

- Spontaneous learning often happens in a richly resourced environment such as this and is every bit as valuable as planned learning. It requires practitioners to put active learning experiences at the start of the assessment process and assess the learning that emerges rather than start from the tick list of assessments and try to think of ways to teach them.

- Children will, in fact, score more highly if observed learning through play as they are motivated, relaxed and engaged. (See 'spontaneous play', p. 17.) ☉

Effective practice

- Resources are key to play provision. They must be accessible, fit for purpose and capable of being used flexibly in ways of children's choosing.

- Staff must also be flexible about the roles they adopt in supporting children's imaginative play – not too overbearing so that children lose the ownership of the script yet available to keep the learning challenging yet achievable. This is no easy task, and new practitioners may need tutoring and support to get the balance just right. (See 'children's ownership', p. 15.)

Planning

In planning a holistic topic such as this, it is important to plan across all areas of the curriculum. Cooking, music, outdoor play, stories, writing, counting and construction play can all be linked to the spider. This helps children to think creatively and laterally. But beware, only make these connections if they occur naturally and do not be tempted to link all learning to the spider for weeks on end.

Resourcing

- The idea of making webs in wool or painting them may intrigue children.

- Making cameras available to photograph webs and providing photos and drawings of different spiders and their webs will provide children with ways of extending their interest

- Time will be needed for staff to answer all the letters sent to the spider.

Carle, E. (1996) *The Very Busy Spider,* London: Puffin.

The EYFS principles

As children can join this learning experience at a range of levels, it caters well for each child's individual interests and learning needs. All of the children, therefore, feel that they can access the learning that is offered which helps to develop their sense of belonging. 'There is something here for me' is a key feeling that young children need to experience as a part of believing that 'school learning' is something they can engage with. The feeling of belonging and mastery orientation will offer them some protection from disaffection later on in their school career. (See 'mastery learner', p. 9 and 'adult's role', p. 21.) The staff in this nursery have achieved the balance between supporting children's ideas yet extending learning by adding ideas and by drawing in parents to what is intrinsically an interesting project.

Bibliography

Ball, A. C. (1994) *The Importance of Early Learning (Startright Report).* Appendix C, London: Royal Society of Arts.

Browne, E. (1995) *Handa's Surprise,* London: Walker.

Bruce, T. (1991) *Time to Play in Early Childhood Education,* London: Hodder & Stoughton.

Bruce, T. (2004) *Cultivating Creativity,* London: Hodder & Stoughton.

Burningham, J. (1994) *Time to Get Out of the Bath, Shirley,* London: Red Fox.

Carle, E. (1996) *The Very Busy Spider,* London: Puffin.

Cousins, J. (1999) *Listening to Four Year Olds,* London: The National Early Years Network.

Dahlberg, G. (1995) 'Everything Has a Beginning and Everything Is Dangerous: Some Reflections on the Reggio Emilia Experience', paper given at an international seminar Nostalgia del Futuro in honour of Loris Malaguzzi, Milan.

Department for Education and Skills (DfES) (1999) *All Our Futures,* London: National Advisory Committee on Creative and Cultural Education.

Department for Education and Skills (DfES) (2004), *Every Child Matters,* London: DfES.

Department for Education and Skills (DfES) (2007) *Early Years Foundation Stage,* London: DfES.

Donaldson, Juliet and Scheffler, Alex (2001) *Room on the Broom,* Basingsoke: Macmillan.

Duffy, B. (1998) *Supporting Creativity and Imagination in the Early Years,* Buckingham: Open University Press.

Dweck, C. (1998) *Self-Theories: Their Role in Motivation, Personality and Development,* London: Taylor & Francis.

Elfer, P., Goldschmied, E., and Selleck, D. (2003) *Key Persons in the Nursery. Building Relationships for Quality Provision,* London: David Fulton.

Goddard Blythe, Sally (2000) 'Mind and Body', *Nursery World,* June.

Gretz, Susanna (1981) *Teddy Bear's Moving Day,* London: Ernest Benn.

Hughes, S. (1993) *Dogger,* London: Red Fox.

Inkpen, Mick (2000) *Kipper's Toy Box,* London: Hodder.

Laevers, Ferre (1994) *Leuven Involvement Scale,* Leuven: Katholieke Universiteit.

Malaguzzi, L. (1998a) 'History, Ideas and Basic Philosophy: An Interview with Lella Gandini', in C. Edwards, L. Gansini and G. Foreman (eds), *The Hundred Languages of Children: The Reggio Emilia Approach – Advanced Reflections,* Greenwich, Conn. and London: Ablex.

Malaguzzi, L. (1998b) 'Hundred Languages of Children', in C. Edwards, L. Gansini and G. Foreman (eds), *The Hundred Languages of Children: The Reggio Emilia Approach – Advanced Reflections,* Greenwich, Conn. and London: Ablex.

Maslow, A. H. (1943) 'A Theory of Human Motivation,' *Psychological Review,* 50: 370–96.

May, P. (2000) 'Water Play in Early Years Settings,' unpublished MA, Oxford Brookes University.

May, P., Ashford, E. and Bottle, G. (2006) *Sound Beginnings,* London: David Fulton.

National Advisory Committee on Creative and Cultural Education (1999) *All Our Futures: Creativity, Culture and Education,* London: Department for Education and Employment.

Nutbrown, C. (1994) *Threads of Thinking,* London: Paul Chapman.

Peers Early Education Partnership (PEEP) (2001) *Learning Together With Babies,* Oxford: PEEP.

Petri, Pat (2005) 'Extending "Pedagogy"', *Journal of Education for Teaching,* 31 (4): 293.

Piaget, J. (1973) *To Understand Is to Invent: The Future of Education,* New York: Grossman.

Sendak, M. (1967) *Where the Wild Things Are,* London: Bodley Head.

Shore, Rima (1997) *Rethinking the Brain,* New York: Families and Work Institute.

Sylva, K., Melhuish, E. C., Sammons, P., Siraj-Blatchford, I. and Taggart, B. (2003) *The Effective Provision of Preschool Education Project: Findings from the Preschool period,* London: Institute of Education.

Vygotsky, L. (1978) 'Interactions Between Learning and Development', in *Mind in Society,* trans. M. Cole, Cambridge, Mass.: Harvard University Press.

Wood, D. J., Bruner, J. S. and Ross, G. (1976) 'The Role of Tutoring in Problem Solving', *Journal of Child Psychology and Psychiatry,* 17: 89–100.